How Prayer Impacts Lives

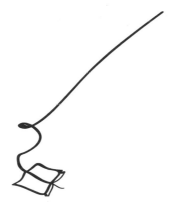

41 Christians and their Conversations with God

Contributors include:
John Piper
Allan M. Harman
Ann Benton
Carine Mackenzie
Roger Carswell
David Robertson
David C. Searle
Robin Sydserff
Rebecca VanDoodewaard
Dorothy Patterson
Steve Brady
Wallace Benn

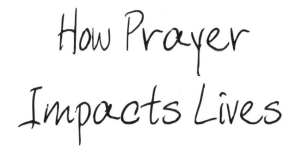

How Prayer Impacts Lives

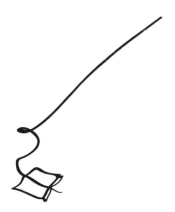

41 Christians and their Conversations with God

Edited by
Catherine Mackenzie

CHRISTIAN FOCUS

Copyright © 2013 Christian Focus Publications

paperback ISBN 978-1-78191-131-0
epub ISBN 978-1-78191-250-8
mobi ISBN 978-1-78191-251-5

Published in 2013
by
Christian Focus Publications,
Geanies House, Fearn, Ross-shire,
IV20 1TW, Scotland, United Kingdom.
www.christianfocus.com

Cover design by Daniel van Straaten

Printed by Bell and Bain, Glasgow

Contents

Adrian Reynolds

Adrian Reynolds is Director of Ministry for the Proclamation Trust and also serves as honorary Associate Minister of East London Tabernacle. He is married to Celia and they have three school-age daughters. They live in East London. Before moving to London, Adrian served as pastor of a Baptist Church in Hampshire.

I'd been a Christian some time before anyone really explained prayer to me. Although it seems a long time ago now, I'm sure that I'd been praying before that time. But when the reality of what prayer *really* is dawned upon me, my Christian life was transformed. Most importantly, some wonderful saint (sorry, but I simply cannot remember who!) showed me that my prayers were only half the story.

The wise advice I received had two parts. First, do not disconnect prayer from Scripture. God speaks in his Word. It's there I know him, know about him, know what he is like, what he likes (and dislikes) and where he reveals his glorious purposes for the world. It's there, fundamentally, that he speaks. Prayer without the Word is a one way street; the kind of conversation where only one person speaks and the other can't get a word in edgewise. I wouldn't like that kind of conversation with any of my friends; why should I want it with the King of kings and Lord of lords?

The second piece of advice I received was to make prayer a response to the Word of God. The two should not just be connected, but I should let God speak first. If I ever meet the Queen (an unlikely occurrence, unless we should unintentionally find ourselves both watching Arsenal[1] one Saturday afternoon), I would certainly let her speak first. Similarly, my prayer is best when it is a response to the God who speaks, whose Son has the name 'The Word of God'.

Practically, this changes my prayers. Without God's voice, my prayers are small and self-centred. With God's Word, my prayers are more likely to be big and Christ-centred. That's true whether I read the prayers of the Bible (the Psalms or Paul's prayers for example) or the truths that the Word of God communicates to my heart.

How can a prayer time be silent and dismal if the Word of God is taking root in my heart and the Spirit of the living God is making the Son of God beautiful to me? After twenty plus years of marriage, my wife still takes my breath away and when I see her, I want to praise her and tell her how wonderful she is. How much more so for the Wonderful Counsellor! As Scripture reveals him, how can I remain silent?

I even try to apply this to those moments where I'm crying out with prayers of immediate anguish. In times of trouble, even David, the great pray-er of the Bible, knows that his prayers must be informed by the character of God. 'Save me, O God, by your name' for 'Surely God is my help; the Lord is the one who sustains me' (Psalm 54:1, 4 NIV). A confident prayer is one spoken out to God using the truths of who he is.

As you get to know Scripture better and better, this does not mean that we need to pray with a Bible physically in our hands (though it can help). Take a phrase or idea and work through it in your mind; let it sink into your heart; make your words a response (our forefathers used to call this biblical meditation).

Prayer belongs with the Word and the Word informs prayer and it was in discovering these vital truths that my prayer life was transformed.

---

[1] Arsenal Football Club play in the British Premier League.

Alasdair and Hilary Cameron

Alasdair and Hilary Cameron are retired C.L.C. Missionaries. Alasdair has served in British Guyana, London and Chatham. Hilary (née Bell) was brought up in Belfast. She was a nurse and missionary with C.L.C. for over 50 years and trained at Redcliffe Bible College in London.

What is prayer? It is a living communication with an awesome God who answers what is best for you as he sees life's bigger picture. Prayer is important. Read Ephesians 6:18:

And pray in the Spirit on all occasions with all kinds of prayers and requests. With this in mind, be alert and always keep on praying for all the Lord's people (NIV).

Now read Matthew 6:9-18 NIV:

> *This, then, is how you should pray:*
> *'Our Father in heaven,*
> *hallowed be your name,*
> *your kingdom come,*
> *your will be done,*
> *on earth as it is in heaven.*
> *Give us today our daily bread.*
> *And forgive us our debts,*
> *as we also have forgiven our debtors.*

> *And lead us not into temptation,*
> *but deliver us from the evil one.*

For if you forgive other people when they sin against you,
your heavenly Father will also forgive you. But if you do
not forgive others their sins, your Father will not forgive
your sins. When you fast, do not look sombre as the
hypocrites do, for they disfigure their faces to show oth-
ers they are fasting. Truly I tell you, they have received
their reward in full. But when you fast, put oil on your
head and wash your face so that it will not be obvious
to others that you are fasting, but only to your Father,
who is unseen; and your Father, who sees what is done in
secret, will reward you (NIV).

We learned very early in our Christian walk, the importance of
prayer through reading the Bible and books like Rees Howells'
Intercessors, and books by George Müller, C.T. Studd, Hudson
Taylor, Andrew Murray and Tozer.

Reading caused us both to understand that prayer needed
to be earnest, persistent, consistent and that there was warfare
involved. The enemy doesn't want us communicating with God.
These days we need to get back to prayer in our churches and
homes.

Alasdair experienced it at a prayer meeting at the WEC
Bible College in Glasgow; Friday night 'Prayer Battery' as it
was called. Extracts were read out from missionary letters
using the same format every week. Letters from Europe first,
then Africa, India, the Far East, South America then the
United Kingdom. After each section there was a time of prayer
when people were free to join in, but they had to be short
and to the point. This was followed by open prayer time. Lots
of people participated and sometimes you could hardly get a
word in! How exciting it was, a week or two later, to hear of
answered prayer!

At these Mission Prayer meetings we learned to pray out
loud in a group, but the words we used didn't concern others
– we were all in prayer together for the lost; for Christian
workers worldwide or in the U.K. for needs; for Governments;

for teachers; etc. It was alive and in no way boring. We came to our all-knowing God who wanted us to bring praise, worship and needs to him.

When Alasdair and I married in 1964, we also actively communicated with God in our marriage and then later with our children, holding onto God in prayer regarding issues that concerned us. Sometimes the answers were immediate, at other times we had to wait and realise that God has this bigger picture. We had to pray and depend on God for our food, clothing, personal finance and church life. Later when we had four children and ran the Mission Headquarters we saw God provide food on the table every day – sometimes at the last minute, but always there. It was exciting, day by day, proving God's faithfulness through prayer.

As our children grew, there was schooling to consider, and all the needs of a family of four. We had to trust in an almighty God. Faith and prayers ran together as a major part of our lives. Praise God He supplied! We could tell you story after story of this.

To really grow and maintain your walk and joy in the Lord you need to keep reading the Word and praying about everything. This brings you the grace to walk, day by day, and enjoy Him. The opportunities He gives to love and care for others and to preach Christ crucified, never cease to amaze us.

Yes, God answers prayer!

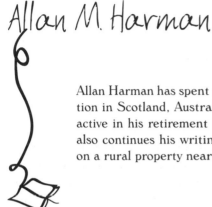

Allan M. Harman

Allan Harman has spent many years in theological education in Scotland, Australia, Korea and the U.S.A. He is active in his retirement in preaching and lecturing, and also continues his writing ministry. He and his wife live on a rural property near the city of Geelong, Australia.

My earliest recollection of prayer is at family worship. Twice a day, morning and evening, my father read a passage of Scripture and then we knelt while he prayed. We as children knew that prayer was an important part of our parents' lives. It did not become important to us until we were brought to trust in the Lord Jesus as teenagers.

Family worship, including prayer, was the generally accepted evangelical practice when I became a Christian. I lived in Sydney during student days in a Christian home. In Edinburgh during theological studies I stayed in the home of a wonderful Christian widow. At the evening meal she would often ask me what we had been discussing at college that day, and we would have a conversation about it. Later in the evening the Bible was read and we knelt. All in the home that evening were expected to pray. Ever since our marriage, my wife and I have carried on the same practice of family devotions.

We don't just pray at times of family prayer. There are many times in the day that call for a short word of prayer. We may go and visit someone in hospital. Sometimes ill patients will simply grip my hand and say, 'Pray with me'.

From the time of my conversion, I have attended weekly prayer meetings at the congregations with which I have been attached. The first time I ever attempted to preach was at one of them. These prayer meetings are an integral part of a fellowship's life, as we bring our corporate requests to the Lord. The time of prayer helps to confirm our common commitment to him, and also our sense of dependence on his sovereign will. It is, in my opinion, a necessary part of congregational practice.

In my own working life I have been a pastor and teacher in theological colleges. I could not have carried on my work without knowing that I could go to the throne of grace and ask for help. I needed wisdom, and turning to God in prayer was also a recognition of my own needs, and also a necessary action before I could minister to others. Paul's instruction to the elders at Ephesus to guard themselves (Acts 20:28) remains a reminder to those of us who are in full-time Christian ministry that we need to pray constantly that God will keep us and make us fruitful in our service for him.

This has been particularly so in relation to my work in preaching from the Bible, teaching it to students, and writing on it. Each day as I begin writing on my current commentary project, I pray. This is first of all a recognition that the things of the Spirit are spiritually discerned. Even a regenerated mind needs divine assistance in understanding what is written. I also ask for help in explaining what the Scripture means so that, by my exposition, readers may be led into a fuller knowledge of God's truth.

Christians have various ways of reminding themselves of the need for daily prayer. Dr Andrew Bonar of Glasgow (1810-1892) had a framed saying on his desk. It read: 'He who has prayed well has completed half his day's work'. How true that is!

Andrew Quigley

Andrew Quigley is an Irishman who has been minister of the Airdrie Reformed Presbyterian Church of Scotland since 1994. He and his wife Heather have six children.

What is Christianity? Well you could define it in a number of ways, but in essence Christianity is the restoration of man's broken relationship with God, by God, for God's glory.

Man was created in God's image to have an unfettered, eternal relationship with Him. But that's not the way it turned out. The reality is much different. That relationship which was to be the source of our unmitigated earthly joy, the well-spring of our eternal delight, was ripped to shreds in a few disastrous minutes in beautiful Eden. As a result of Adam's pride-filled rebellion, life is a daily battle marked by angst-ridden bitterness. It's often a lonely experience. An aimless wandering of perpetual futility. A vapour, a passing mist, here today and gone tomorrow. God, our Creator, describes our lives using terms like: darkness, slavery, death... . That's the reality of your life, and of my life, or is it? As you flick through the pages of this book are you doing so as one who has experienced the life-changing power of God in your life? Have you, by God's grace, been set free from your personal slavery to sin through the death of God's only Son, Jesus Christ? If not, there is only one prayer that you can and must pray, 'God be merciful to me, I confess I am a sinner. I do repent. Please give me the faith to believe in the Lord Jesus Christ!' If you have been born again then what a glorious position you and I are in. We are now living, because of the wonder of God's love, in a restored relationship with Him. But let me ask you a question. What does that restored relationship mean to you? Do have an insatiable desire for that relationship to be a real and vital one? Are you really genuinely desperate for it to be a relationship in which you live and breathe?

That's where prayer comes into it for me. I have to be honest, I can't cope. I am a married man with six children (one of them married), and there is never a day goes by that I am not acutely aware of my failures in every one of those relationships. I am the minister of a small congregation of mainly new converts, and I know only too well from past failures that their needs are greater than my ability to meet them. Too often I find myself having to apologise for not getting items on my 'to do list' done. I desperately wish I wasn't, but I am an active sinner. I think thoughts I shouldn't. I use words that hurt. I do things which I am truly ashamed of. I shout too often, sometimes cry, and laugh, but not often enough. I can be quick to judge. At some point during the year I wrestle with deep rooted depression due to overwork and the frequent failure to take a proper Sabbath day's rest. The most disheartening thing of all though is that I never seem to learn, and if and when I do, it's only after years of chastening.

Plain and simple, prayer for me is about coping, no it goes further than just coping, it's about conquering. Prayer is about accessing the forgiveness and love of God. The forgiveness and love which I crave and so desperately need. The forgiveness which enables me to keep my messed up head straight and my wandering heart engaged. The love which drives out the fear in my life and secures for me the daily desire to obey His commands. Prayer is about engaging in a conversation with my Heavenly Father which begins with me listening to what He has to say about Himself, my family, His Church, myself, and this sin-sick world in which we live. Prayer, my concrete, tangible

communion with my Father is what keeps me going day after
day. Without being melodramatic, without prayer I would have
long since shrivelled up and died. How can I be so definite
about it? Because I know how close I have come to shrivelling
up and dying when I haven't been listening and then crying out
to Him in prayer.

The man who wrote Psalm 91 puts it brilliantly. He paints
a chilling picture of a battlefield. The carnage is devastating.
It is all encompassing, there is nowhere to hide from it. The
incoming fire is relentless from the sky and from every possible
angle on the ground. It is incessant. It is never ending. It is
being waged day and night. When the sun rises, the battle
is on, when the moon and stars shine, the battle is being
engaged. The casualties are numbered daily in their thousands.
The wounded and the dead mount up. Is anywhere safe in the
midst of such devastating and unrelenting brutality? There is!
In the shadow of the Almighty. 'When he calls to me, I will
answer him, I will be with him in trouble; I will rescue him and
honour him. With long life I will satisfy him and show him my
salvation' (Ps. 91:14-16 RSV).

But how can you be sure? How can you be sure that if you
call on God, that He will listen? You only have one life, and it's
incredibly short. The battle is not a game, the casualties are
real, and we can so easily become entangled and quickly find
ourselves numbered among them. But 'we have confidence to
enter the holy place by the blood of Jesus,' (Heb. 10:19 RSV)
and 'the eyes of the Lord are on the righteous and his ears are
open to their prayer' (1 Pet. 3:12 RSV). You and I can be sure
that God will talk with us because His Son, our Saviour the
Lord Jesus, has opened the door for us into the very presence
of the Father.

As God addresses my life, in particular through His Psalms,
the praise and prayer book of his people, I am drawn to speak,
having first listened, and this is prayer. In this praying I am
enabled to cope, even conquer, as God, in His own time,
continues to conform me into the image of His Son – His
ultimate purpose for my life!

Andy and Jennifer Gill

Andy and Jennifer Gill are both secondary school teachers from Fife. In their book 'Love Oliver' they tell the story of their first son, Oliver, who was born with a very rare form of cancer. Despite smiling his way through intensive chemotherapy, he passed away peacefully at home, aged just twenty four weeks old. Andy and Jennifer have recently been blessed with their second son, Micah. Their charity, LoveOliver, has already raised over £120,000 for childhood cancer research and support for families.

As our baby son, Oliver, passed away in our arms early on Christmas morning 2010, aged just twenty-four weeks old, we could not help but wonder why God had not answered our desperate prayers for healing and the prayers of thousands of people across the world in the way we all so longed for. Why had God not intervened to heal Oliver from the rare and aggressive form of cancer he had been born with? At the same time as wrestling with these obvious questions, we have also been comforted by an overwhelming sense of peace that confirms it is all for a good reason.

During Oliver's illness, people across the world were moved to pray for him and for us, and this led to us experiencing the effects of prayer in a new and powerful way. We would never have thought any peace, far less a peace so strong, could be experienced in the fiery furnace or the lions' den. However, as we have faced our own fiery furnace and faced the darkest days of our lives, we have come to know God's peace which truly does pass all understanding. We know without a doubt that our story would be very different if it were not for the power of prayer.

Even since Oliver passed away, the continuing prayers of God's people have helped us to stay positive. We have set up a successful charity, named LoveOliver, in his memory. We have also been blessed with the birth of Oliver's little brother, Micah. We firmly believe God is continuing to use Oliver's life and story in amazing ways, to His glory. As a result, much needed research into childhood cancer is advancing, families are being supported further and Oliver's beautiful smile and life story are continuing to touch people's lives.

We longed for Oliver to be healed and to see him grow up. Even though we know we will one day see him again, we long for him to still be here and every day we have to commit ourselves to trusting God's ways even though we do not understand them. They are definitely the best. They are hard and painful and not what we would choose for ourselves, but we know we can trust they are somehow right.

Thinking of everything we have faced and continue to deal with, it often feels very surreal. We know we could not have got through any of it in our own strength. Many people have remarked on how strong, positive and together we have been throughout everything, and we know this is because people have prayed for us so faithfully. God may not have answered our prayers in the way we wanted Him to, but each day he has given us the strength to be able to fulfil the plans He has for us. Knowing that prayer has equipped us with everything we have needed to be able to cope and stay strong on our journey with Oliver, our faith and confidence in God, prayer and His plans have been deepened more than ever before. We know how hard and evil this world can be. We know that one day we will rejoice in Heaven, reunited with Oliver and serving our Saviour, free from pain and sadness. We know that until then prayer is an essential and powerful weapon which we need to enable us to face each day.

Prayer is about completely committing every situation in your life to God and to His will, and being prepared to accept whatever His answer may be, trusting that it is the best for your life. It helps you to live life with the confidence that no matter what happens, God provides you with everything you need for doing His will. It helps you to be able to give thanks and say, 'Blessed be Your name when the sun's shining down on me' and 'Blessed be Your name on the road marked with suffering'. A beautiful song called 'Blessings' written by Laura Story says:

> What if Your blessings come through raindrops?
> What if Your healing comes through tears?
> What if a thousand sleepless nights are what it
>   takes to know You're near?
> What if trials of this life are Your mercies in disguise?

These words remind us that God is good all the time and can be praised in the storm. Prayer helps you to get to know Him and to deepen your faith in His plans for you, no matter how hard they may sometimes be to understand. Philippians 4:6-7(NLT) says: 'Don't worry about ANYTHING; instead, pray about EVERYTHING. Tell God what you need, and thank him for ALL he has done. THEN you will experience God's peace, which exceeds ANYTHING we can understand.' We now know how true these words are.

A Drought and an Umbrella

There was a severe drought some years ago in the northern part of England. The situation became so severe that if it would not rain within a week, the crops would be totally lost. Due to this urgent need, it was decided to have a special prayer service for rain in one of the local churches. As the minister of this congregation was approaching the church, he saw a little girl ahead of him carrying an umbrella. He caught up with the girl and asked her, 'My little girl, why are you carrying an umbrella to church on such a hot day?' Turning and looking into his face, the girl answered, 'We are going to ask God to send rain today. I want to be ready.' The minister testified in his sermon that the faith of this girl put him to shame.

Taken from *How God Used a Drought and an Umbrella* by Joel Beeke and Diana Kleyn, published by Christian Focus Publications. ISBN: 978-1-85792-818-1

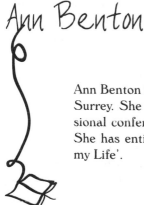

Ann Benton

Ann Benton is married to a pastor and lives in Guildford, Surrey. She is a mother, grandmother, writer and occasional conference speaker, particularly on family issues. She has entitled this article 'How Prayer has Impacted my Life'.

The essence of prayer is dependence on God. I read that sentence somewhere some years ago and it has stayed with me. It sums up how prayer has impacted my life.

I could tell of extraordinary answers to prayer, by which I mean times when things turned out precisely as I had hoped and prayed they would, sometimes with extraordinary speed and in surprising ways. But that would not be an honest overall picture of my forty-four years of Christian life. There are many prayers I have prayed for years, even decades, and I still wait and watch for God to work. I have been bewildered sometimes by God's apparent failure to do as I asked – when it seemed such a good idea at the time and I was convinced that for God to act in the way I prescribed would really glorify his name. In other words God has seemed as often to say 'no' as to say 'yes' to my prayers.

But God taught me about dependence on him. I suppose I am an organising sort of person, who likes to plan her way out of any crisis, who thinks that most problems can be solved by hard work and a positive attitude. I had to learn that is not the case. And like all the most significant lessons of life, they are learned in hard times, when things are not turning out well either for me or for those I care about.

Luke records in his Gospel (Luke 11) how Jesus taught what is known as 'The Lord's Prayer' in answer to his disciples' request that he would teach them to pray. At that time Jesus also told a story, which I think his original listeners would have found amusing. It concerns a man who was caught out with an empty larder when an unexpected guest arrived. This is a situation I would really hate, as an organising sort of person. The expectation of hospitality is integral to Middle Eastern culture. But even I, with a far less generous background culture, would be embarrassed not to be able to offer an old friend tea and toast. I have read that in Jesus' day it was common practice for homesteads within the village to take it in turns to bake all the village bread on any given day. So for the desperate man to knock up the baker-of-the-day was a reasonable course of action even if at an unreasonable time. And the procedure might have met with a grumpy response, but it also achieved the desired end-product. The man got his bread.

Now, God is not grumpy. He has the resources we need and it is impossible to catch him napping. Note to self: instead of trying always to manage on my own, run to God who is neither tired nor grumpy, and ask him. The essence of prayer is dependence on God.

Another tip on prayer which has proved useful is about using the Lord's Prayer as a pattern. I am no prayer heroine or warrior, just a learner still, but I always come back to this. Pray first and foremost for God's name to be honoured, God's kingdom to be extended, God's will to be done. Whatever is on your mind when you come to pray, you can't go wrong with that approach. And such a beginning rightly centres your mind away from yourself.

But that same prayer which Jesus taught also relates to the personal and the human. It is right to pray for your physical needs and to recognise that every meal you eat comes from God's hand. No less necessary on a daily basis is forgiveness. The seriousness of sin is underlined in all the descriptions of the Old Testament sacrifices. Even unintentional, unconscious sins are serious, let alone the ones with malicious forethought. But those sacrifices are also pointing to the fact that forgiveness is possible as well as necessary. And the ultimate sacrifice of Jesus' death makes forgiveness a guaranteed result for those who will ask. The admission of my dependence on God for daily cleansing and the act of asking for it also gets me off my high horse with regard to other people. I need that.

The Lord's prayer ends with a request for protection. This world is a dangerous and disappointing place. And not all the dangers are outside of me. Not only are all Christians in a war, it is also true to say that they are the battlefield. I am kidding myself if I think I can walk the road to heaven without help. So I pray to God every day for him to give me his protection for one more day.

The essence of prayer is dependence on God. And perhaps that is also the essence of the Christian life. And if prayer doesn't always change things, as far as the human eye can see, it changes the person who prays. And in my case, that has been a good thing.

What is Prayer?

D. L. Moody, the famous American evangelist, was preaching in Edinburgh one day to a large crowd of children. In order to get their attention he asked them a question: 'What is prayer?' He wasn't really expecting an answer, but to his astonishment many little hands shot up all over the room. So Moody asked one young lad to speak up. The boy stood up and confidently replied, 'Prayer is an offering up of our desires unto God for things agreeable to His will, in the name of Christ, with confession of our sins and thankful acknowledgment of His mercies.' Moody's response was, 'Thank God, my boy, that you were born in Scotland.'

Barbara Giarratana

Barbara Giarratana has spent the last twenty plus years raising her three children in rural New Jersey. Now empty nesters, she and her husband, Bill, live in North Carolina and await their first grandchild. For over ten years they have been partners in their own company that provides fund-raising services for Christian non-profit organizations and sales promotion for Christian publishers.

Some people may wonder if prayer "works", as if it is a magic potion or set of words that have power. News Flash: They have *no* power of their own! And that is the beauty of prayer. The words spoken in prayer have no power except by the fact of WHO the prayer is being spoken to. And to that end that tiny little prayer of, "Please help me" has the power to move mountains. I know and I've seen.

What things come to mind when I think about prayer? Well, I remember that prayer is a privilege that we have here on earth. It is a life-line to the throne of God, to the Holy of holies. I never forget where I am entering as I begin my prayer whether for myself or others.

I also remember when praying for someone not to get involved with all the details, but simply lift the person up to His throne where God sees, knows and loves all. Once there the Holy Spirit brings to my lips the prayer that is to be prayed for that person. I surrender and commit the person or situation to the Lord and leave it there at His feet. When I think of someone, I pray for them always thanking God for bringing them to my attention. When I've been woken up from a deep sleep with someone on my mind; I pray right then for this person and am filled with joy that God would call me to be a part of His prayer team for this person.

A heart of thanksgiving and praise is central to prayer. Recently, praying for a two year old with an aggressive type of cancer, I included in my prayer thanksgiving and praise because I know that God has a plan not only for this child, but for her family to draw closer to Him. Some might think it odd to be thanking God for such a terrible calamity, but we must trust God and know that whatever happens, happens because He loves us and will use the situation for His glory.

We must be prayer sensitive so that we may be called upon by God to intercede for others. Not knowing that I had just had the last conversation with my mother, who did not have a relationship with God, I lifted her physical wellbeing up to the Lord and started to go to bed. I had shared the gospel with my mother for over thirty years and she rejected Jesus as her Savior, preferring to work her way to heaven herself. Upon entering my bed after hanging up the phone with her I clearly heard: "You are not finished praying for her." I paused from pulling up the covers as I grasped what I just heard. I lay my head down and prayed for my mother's salvation. My mother never woke up, but I know that God ministered to her as her sleep transformed into the process of dying. There, where God had her undivided attention, she was ministered to by the Holy Spirit. And, of course, this could have happened without my prayers; but by His love He included me because He knew I would need this assurance of the Holy Spirit ministering to my mother. *How Great Is Our God!!*

I couldn't live without prayer. In times of sickness, in times of stress, in times of financial difficulties, in times of grief and calamity we go to Him. He is there to work out these things in our lives as He is committed to care for us. But prayer isn't just about petitioning the Lord, it is also about worshiping Him. Setting aside worries and saying, "You Lord are more important than all of these things put together." We must never lose sight of WHO we are praying to. No, it is not our words that have power to change lives or situations, but it is WHO we are praying to. Thankfully, it is our meager words of praise and thanksgiving that rise up to the Lord as a sweet fragrance.

In giving all glory and honor to the One who loves me and loves you, I will share that I've seen tremendous answers to prayer. I was supposed to have had double knee replacements over five years ago and sought the Lord through prayer. Today I can walk without any aid and without pain because God heard my prayers and healed both my knees. I've prayed over a meager amount of food to provide for a growing family and even unexpected guests and miraculously have been able to feed all.

If you think God isn't listening, think again. Just because a situation doesn't turn out the way you want or think it should, doesn't mean that your prayer wasn't or won't be answered. After all, you don't really know what is best in every situation, but God does. Trust Him, Go to Him, Love Him and Speak to Him. This is prayer. It's not complicated. Just do it.

An Instinctive Cry

The baby cries, instinctively; and the born-again person instinctively prays, crying to God in dependence, hope and trust as a child to his father. The gospel which he received and to which he responded by embracing Christ as his Saviour and Lord promised him adoption into God's family (Gal. 4:4f.), and now it is his nature to treat God as his Father, bringing to Him all his own felt needs and desires. We (believers, the regenerate ones) 'received the Spirit of sonship. And by him we cry, "Abba, Father"' (Rom. 8:15 NIV). The new Christian's prayers are honest and heartfelt, as children's cries for help always are, and though as he matures, prayer may become harder (this does happen) it never ceases to be the most natural activity in which he engages. Constantly to look up to God as your Father in heaven and to talk to Him in and from your heart is thus a sign of being regenerate.

Taken from *18 Words* by J.I. Packer, published by Christian Focus Publications. ISBN: 978-1-84550-327-7

Cameron Tallach

Cameron is sixty-eight years old and a retired GP living on the Isle of Skye. He has been married to Ishbel for forty-four years with three grown-up children and two grandchildren. He spent twenty-eight years in the Far East, mostly in Hong Kong as a medical missionary; something he says was 'a great privilege!'

Here are two abiding memories about prayer from when I was a little boy: One is of me standing outside the door of the back room in our manse in Kames, hearing my mother's groans as she prayed for her boys. The other, of my great concern because I had disturbed a bird's nest with chicks in it and had heard that the mother bird would not then come back to care for her young. Mum prayed about that too, that God would bring the mother bird back to take care of her chicks. Two early memories, both pointing me to a God who cares for little things and for little people. Bringing up children in an atmosphere of sincere, loving prayer is surely a powerful aid to their trusting God.

Sometimes prayer is mechanical, performing a duty, dry, not very interesting. Even then I find that taking time to persevere, being honest before God and asking him for help, brings a gradual melting of spirit – God draws closer and there is real fellowship. Other times the fellowship is there from the beginning, especially if a portion of Scripture has opened up with fresh insight – God speaking before I do. For prayer should not be one-directional. Fellowship surely is the heart of it. So we should pray with our ears open as well as our mouths. Wasn't this what Jesus sought when he went off on his own to speak to his Father in heaven? Observing his example and longing for deeper fellowship, we can ask like his disciples, 'Lord, teach us to pray.'

The Shorter Catechism says that we are '…in our prayers to praise him'. Personally, I want to, yet have found it difficult. However, the Psalms can help us greatly here. And I have also found it helpful, even refreshing, to thank God for the things he has done. Read the Scriptures, learn again his mighty works – in Creation, at the Red Sea, throughout the life of Jesus, in his death and resurrection – and simply say, 'Thank you, Lord.' Should we not also have our own personal history of God's mighty works and the kindness, mercy and grace he has shown to us? Perhaps we should be writing our own psalms in praise of what he has done for us.

Through prayer we come to the throne of grace, where God, our Father, sits, Jesus Christ his Son at his right hand. We are introduced to the great company of forgiveness, welcome, acceptance and love. On our part we are to show love, trust, reverence and humility. From that throne, almighty God says to his little child, 'What do you want ME to do for you?'

Lord, help me to use the opportunity!

When we pray, God is not obliged, even by his own word, to answer us at any particular time. In Luke 18:1-8, Jesus warns us that God may delay his answer. So beware of growing impatient. The Canaanite woman in Matthew chapter 15 is a wonderful example of persevering prayer. She had a deep conviction that Jesus had the power to help her. She kept coming till she got the answer she wanted.

The question is, are our prayers an expression of our heart's desires or merely indifferent requests? God knows. George Müller spoke of praying for forty years – with expectation – for someone's salvation!

Unanswered prayer can be painful, perplexing. I identify with a Christian who commented, 'One of my biggest struggles is unanswered prayer.' We pray for sick people who die, for broken marriages which end in divorce, for deliverance of persecuted Christians and they are executed. We pray against proposed ungodly laws but they are voted through, and for revival but evil seems to prosper. C.S. Lewis spoke of having the door slammed in his face and double bolted on the other side. Where is God in all this? He is still on his throne, and not indifferent. He wants us to know, 'My thoughts are not your thoughts, nor are your ways my ways, says the Lord' (Isaiah 55:8). He knows what he is doing and can see the outcome far better than we can. It still hurts, but we need to trust him and indeed praise him, for it won't be the first time he has used the enemy's apparent success to prosper his own kingdom.

An American businessman who had been very wealthy, with two Cadillacs, a huge house and many other valuable possessions, met an elderly lady who regularly attended a nearby prayer meeting. For some reason she took an interest in him and began to pray for him. His business failed, and one after another he had to give up his treasured possessions. Broken and desperate, he called on God and that is how he came to be speaking to us at a Christian men's breakfast in Hong Kong. His advice – 'If you don't want your life turned upside down, avoid elderly ladies who pray!' Of course, from his new perspective, he was really saying, 'Join them'!

God's Sovereignty

Prayer is an essential part of the providence of God, so essential, that you will always find that when God delivers His people, His people have been praying for that deliverance. They tell us that prayer does not affect the Most High, and cannot alter His purposes. We never thought it did; but prayer is a part of the purpose and plan, and a most effective wheel in the machinery of providence.

Charles Spurgeon

Carine Mackenzie

Carine Mackenzie is a children's author. Her talent for retelling Bible stories has meant that children from all over the world have been given the opportunity to discover Jesus Christ for themselves. Carine is a grandmother and lives in Inverness, Scotland.

One of my earliest memories is hearing my father praying at family worship. Every day after breakfast and before going to bed, the whole family would gather together to read from the Bible and sometimes sing a Psalm. We would then kneel at our chairs and my father would lead us in prayer – asking for forgiveness of sins, committing each of us to the Lord's care, thanking him for all his goodness to us, especially for the Saviour, the Lord Jesus. It was an essential part of our daily routine – not a legalistic habit but a useful practice which helped us to focus on what is really important – the amazing privilege of hearing from God's Word and speaking to Him in prayer.

Family prayer time has been a constant in my life – first with my parents and brother and sister, then with my husband and our children. Now there are just the two of us in the home again, but the time of family prayer is very precious – fellowship with the Lord and with each other.

Another early memory concerns the time when I was about five or six years old. I told a lie to Elizabeth, one of my little friends. One day in school she gave me a piece of her chocolate birthday cake. I was so thrilled with it I decided to take it home to show the family. I placed it carefully in my school bag! Of course when I reached home the cake was in bits and my school bag was a mess. The cake was scraped away and disposed of.

'Did you enjoy my cake?' Elizabeth asked the next day.

'Yes, I did,' I replied. 'It tasted lovely.'

I knew that was not true and that lie bothered my conscience. When my mother eventually found out why I was crying, she said, 'Let's tell Jesus about it.' And that's what we did. I told Jesus what I had said and asked for his forgiveness.

Throughout life I have done that so many times – just told Jesus about it – anywhere – any time of day – alone or in a crowd. There is no need to wait till the time of family prayer, or till we go to church – we can speak to the Lord any time. He listens to every problem – a troubled conscience, a health issue, bereavement, worry. There is a great comfort in telling him the problem. There is no need to suggest a solution – he knows what is best and will work all things out for our good. The Lord asks us to cast all our care on him because he cares for us. What peace we find when we do that.

Sometimes we forget to pray, but Jesus never forgets. He is always praying for his people. He 'always lives to make intercession for them' (i.e. those who come to God through Christ) (Hebrews 7:25 NKJV).

Sometimes we cannot express our prayers adequately, all we can do is sigh or groan. But God hears that prayer too. The Holy Spirit helps us and prays for us with groanings which cannot be expressed in words.

It is only because of Jesus Christ and what he has done for us that we can approach God in prayer. Jesus takes our poor prayers and presents them to God the Father.

God always answers prayer. He does not always say 'Yes'. His answer is sometimes, 'Not yet' and sometimes, 'No, I know what is best for you'.

Jesus taught us to pray, 'Your will be done on earth as it is in heaven.' Prayer is not asking God to do what we want but asking God to make us know and agree with his will and purpose. What a marvellous gift.

Catherine Mackenzie

Catherine Mackenzie has grown up amongst books. Today she works as the Children's Editor at Christian Focus Publications in Scotland and has written several biographies for teenagers and young children.

When I was a little girl I began to pray prayers of my own, kneeling by the bed and thinking that I was very good. But my prayers were frequently wide off the mark.

For example, if I was tired and wanted to get under the covers it would be something like, 'Dear God bless everyone in the whole world. Amen.'

At other times, when I wanted to delay having to go to sleep, I would reel off the name of every relative I could think of – and with a family of seventeen cousins that could take a while.

Sometimes the things I prayed for were simply wrong. One night, for some bizarre reason, I thought a flood would be really exciting – so I prayed for that. Our house was on top of a fairly big hill in the middle of town. I'm very glad God did not say yes to that juvenile prayer.

Other times I prayed for things that were right – but my motives were wrong. One evening I was scared of dying. I had heard that it was good to pray, 'God be merciful to me a sinner.' For half an hour or maybe more I prayed that prayer again and again and again. It was as if those words were some sort of talisman. If they were said often enough they would magically take away my fear of death, giving me a first class ticket to heaven. But when I said those words I wasn't praying for mercy and I was not recognising myself as a sinner – so I wasn't really praying at all.

I do remember getting lost one day. It was a silly situation for me to get myself into. Mum had told me to walk on ahead and meet her at the paper-shop. She would come along in the car a few minutes later and pick me up. I heard the words paper-shop but in that little dream world I often occupied as an eight-year-old I went to the grocer's shop instead which was at the other end of the street. I waited and waited and waited. No sign of mum. Distressed and more than a little tearful I made my way home. Mum drove up a few minutes later to find me sobbing on the back step. In between the sobs I had been fervently praying to God – perhaps the first time I had prayed a truly personal prayer in my whole life.

The little red DAF car was the perfect answer to prayer. It was an answered prayer that I could see – bright-red and boxy with my mum inside it. It was one that I could also hear – everyone could hear that car – you could hear it start up from the other end of the street.

Later on in life I started to get a bit bogged down in prayer. I thought I wasn't doing it right. Sometimes I was nervous, at other times just really, really confused. Often I didn't know what to say.

However, during a conversation with my Dad we began to discuss the issues I had with salvation and prayer. I had been thinking about being a Christian for some time. I had even prayed about it to God but again I just wasn't sure if my prayers were good enough. Was I good enough? I think Dad addressed the fact that it was only Jesus who was good enough first, and then he went on to tackle my issue with prayer. He quoted a Bible verse, 'Come now, and let us reason together, saith the LORD: though your sins be as scarlet, they shall be as white as snow' (Isaiah 1:18 KJV). He described prayer as God and I reasoning together – in much the same way that I often reasoned things out with my parents. It was a simple communication-conversation. God was inviting me – I wasn't muscling my way in. God wanted to listen to me and for me to learn from him. He wanted to reason with me. So yes – he knew that I was in a muddle, that my thoughts as well as my words were wrong and sinful – but he wanted to help. Prayer with him was the best place to start.

I think I'd like to close by recommending one particular writer – E.M. Bounds. There is a story that he mentions in his book *The Necessity of Prayer*[1] which I believe is helpful to those of us who feel our prayers are inadequate to say the least.

> *The guests at a certain hotel were being rendered uncomfortable by the repeated strumming on a piano, done by a little girl who possessed no knowledge of music. They complained to the proprietor with a view to having the annoyance stopped. "I am sorry you are annoyed," he said. "But the girl is the child of one of my very best guests. I can scarcely ask her not to touch the piano. But her father, who is away for a day or so, will return tomorrow. You can then approach him, and have the matter set right." When the father returned he found his daughter in the reception-room and, as usual, thumping on the piano. He walked up behind the child and, putting his arms over her shoulders, took her hands in his, and produced some most beautiful music. Thus it may be with us, and thus it will be, some coming day. Just now, we can produce little but clamour and disharmony; but, one day, the Lord Jesus will take hold of our hands of faith and prayer, and use them to bring forth the music of the skies.*

I look forward to that day, to the melody of sinless, perfect prayer and hope to have even just a little flavour of it now.

---

[1] *The Necessity of Prayer* by E.M. Bounds is published by Christian Focus Publications ISBN: 978-1-84550-209-9

David Joy

David Joy is the author of a monthly publication entitled 'Thoughts on the Gospel' which is widely distributed by e-mail and by post. He is a member of the Associated Presbyterian Church and for many years was a lay preacher throughout the North of Scotland.

While out hill-walking one day my footsteps led me to a wooden bridge which crossed a fast flowing mountain stream. The sun was shining and the area around the bridge was ablaze with colour. As there was a lovely view down the valley below me, I decided to stop there for a while and enjoy the peace.

When I sat down I noticed a spider scurrying across the thick planks of the bridge seemingly intent on getting to the other side. Because there were large gaps between each plank I found myself wondering how far it would get before falling into the stream below. Before long this is what appeared to have happened as the spider disappeared down one of the gaps. A short while later however, it appeared again and carried on its way.

I watched it more closely and the next time it fell I was able to see that the spider had a lifeline – a fine silver thread that held it safely, suspended above the water below. It was this lifeline that not only prevented it from falling into the stream but enabled it to bridge the gaps between the planks on the bridge.

Prayer has been my lifeline. Prayer has been the means of keeping me connected to God. It has brought me peace when my life has been in turmoil. It has lifted my spirits when struggling along the dark valleys of life. It has restored my confidence in God when I have found myself falling prey to Satan's devices. It has given me access to Jesus who always listens and never lets me down. It has at times brought great joy into my heart. Like the spider's lifeline that held it safe in time of need, prayer has brought me security, safety and peace.

I have kept a diary for over fifty years and all through its pages I find entries which record details of prayers that have been answered.

Once I prayed for a friend lost in fearful conditions in the Cairngorm Mountains. A week after he had gone missing, when most people believed he had perished, he was found safe and well, entrenched in a snow hole he had dug for shelter.

On another occasion I found myself burdened with concern for a friend who had been diagnosed with cancer. I prayed for healing and eight years on he is still in remission from the cancer.

For many years I prayed for a man who felt he had no hope of salvation such was the life he had led. Ten minutes before he passed away he confessed that Jesus was his only hope for eternity.

My daughter, when she was a child, once had terrible toothache. As she sat on my knee crying with pain I begged God to take away the toothache. She had no further pain until the day she had the offending tooth removed.

Many of my prayers have been answered but one in particular always comes to mind. Prior to my conversion, my mind was full of doubts concerning the message of salvation and one day I prayed 'Lord help me.' A sermon I heard, later that day, with these words as the main theme, was used to bring me to a saving knowledge of Jesus Christ.

Have all my prayers been answered? The answer must be no for some things as yet await an answer. What can I say then that can do justice to what prayer has done and is doing for me?

Prayer is my lifeline! Perhaps all I need to say is that, like the spider that would have been lost without its lifeline, I would feel lost without mine.

David Robertson

David is a columnist, author, broadcaster and pastor of St. Peter's Free Church of Scotland in Dundee. He is the Director of the Solas Centre for Public Christianity.

The speaker was adamant – 'I don't believe in God because I have never seen or heard of anyone who has experienced answered prayer'. He was an atheist who prided himself in his 'evidence based' scientific approach to life. I was next in turn to speak and basically ripped up my prepared speech to begin by simply responding – 'You have now'. As a Christian for over thirty-five years and a minister for over twenty-five you would of course expect me to believe in prayer – or rather to believe in the One who answers prayer. Over my life I have experienced many answers, questions and responses to prayer. I have wrestled, struggled, practiced and denied prayer. But of one thing I am certain – I am able to write this today because of answered prayer.

In October 2011, I collapsed in a pool of blood outside my church after conducting a wedding. Although spectacular it was not considered to be too serious – a couple of bleeding ulcers should have been easily dealt with by a routine endoscopy procedure. Except that from this point on nothing was routine. Three endoscopies could not stop the bleeding and my lungs

almost drowned in blood. I have little or no recollection of the
several weeks I spent in the Intensive Care Unit in Ninewells
Hospital, Dundee, but I have since been told that three times
I came close to death. The inability to breath, e-coli of the
lung, numerous infections, a haemoglobin rate of 4, and finally
pneumonia all threatened to end my life. My family at one
point were told that there was nothing that the hospital could
do, that I was unlikely to make it through, and that it was now
all up to me. Little wonder that my wife was incredulous – up
to me?! I was comatosed and unable to move, communicate or
do anything. Thankfully it *was* up to someone else.

Of course my family were praying. As were friends and
the church. Apparently even in my delusional state (brought
on by the drugs that had to be administered) I was asking
for prayer. At one point I even wrote that people should be
called to fast and pray between 3 and 4 pm one particular
afternoon. I guess I figured that people could manage to fast
for one hour! But people did pray – and then some. There are
three extraordinary aspects of this that stand out in my mind.
Firstly, on one particular Sunday the whole Free Church were
asked to stop what they were doing and pray at 12 noon for my
recovery. Secondly, I have received many reports from people
to the effect that they would be woken in the middle of the
night with a strong urge to pray for me and could not go back
to sleep until they did so. It seems as though God gave the
burden for prayer and then answered the prayers he inspired.
I am reminded of Augustine's prayer, 'O Lord, command what
you will, and give what you command.'

Sometimes it was difficult for my family to pray. What could
they ask for? How could they express what they felt when they
saw me agitated, in agony and at times in great spiritual and
emotional turmoil? There were no words. Except there were.
God's words. And especially those given to us in the prayer
book of the Bible – the Psalms. They were so precious, real
and emotional. We used them every day. Psalms like Psalm 91
were read or sung to me every night. In fact, the whole time
I was in hospital I did not go to sleep at night without a Psalm.
And as a Presbyterian brought up in a tradition that prayer
should be un-rehearsed and generally not written down, I was

surprised at how helpful I found the prayers in the Anglican Book of Common Prayer.

And the prayers were answered. One night lying in the High Dependency Unit I knew that I was going to get better and that God still had a role for me on this earth. Since then I have lived every day grateful for life and for the particular answer that was given to myself and so many people in answer to prayer. I say particular because of course there could have been other answers. As my son, Andrew, pointed out, 'If Dad dies then that too will be an answer to prayer.' And so it would have been. The atheist cited at the beginning of the passage, upon hearing this, stated that that was not fair because then God wins every way. Indeed He does. And that is totally fair. As a Christian I believe that God works all things together for the good of those who love him – even illness and death. 'Precious in the sight of the Lord is the death of his saints' (Psalm 116:15 KJV). One day I will die – until then I will live on this earth thankful to God that I am living proof that prayer does indeed impact lives.

Constant and Steadfast

Rejoice in hope, be patient in tribulation, be constant in prayer (Rom. 12:12 ESV).

Continue steadfastly in prayer, being watchful in it with thanksgiving (Col. 4:2 ESV).

Take the helmet of salvation, and the sword of the Spirit, which is the word of God, praying at all times in the Spirit, with all prayer and supplication. To that end keep alert with all perseverance, making supplication for all the saints (Eph. 6:17-18 ESV).

David C. Searle

Having served in parishes in Aberdeenshire, Larbert and Northern Ireland, and also directing the work of Rutherford House in Edinburgh, David and his wife Lorna are now retired and enjoying their eight grandchildren. He has entitled his article 'The God of the Impossible'.

I was brought up by parents who believed and constantly proved that God hears and answers prayer. So from an early age I knew about God's gracious ways with those who love and serve him. During the fifty years of my ministry I have experienced for myself his gracious help and intervention in my life.

Early on in my first ministry which was in a rural congregation we felt unable to fix any date for our annual Harvest Thanksgiving. For weeks the rain had been incessant. The year was 1967 and the small farms surrounding the church still used old-fashioned 'binders' which necessitated the corn standing in the fields in 'stooks' to dry out.

A challenge came to me: dare I put God to the test and pray publicly in church for three weeks of good harvesting weather? I had often wondered about praying for good weather because such prayers might be ignoring others who needed rain. But I was seeking to plant an evangelical congregation in an historic rural parish. I was longing for God in some way to accredit my ministry and demonstrate the authority of his Word.

For three successive nights I wrestled with the Lord, crying out to him to guide me in this matter of praying for three weeks of harvest weather. If I prayed publicly and the weather remained wet, then my credibility (and God's honour) would be undermined! The stakes were high.

The following Sunday with my knees feeling like water, I prayed during the service for three weeks of cloudless skies and strong drying winds. A felt silence came upon the congregation; people seemed to stop breathing. The sound of rain beating on the roof made my prayer seem sheer folly. In the 1960s there were no long range forecasts. The weather seemed set to continue to waterlog the fields.

However, the next day dawned with a cloudless sky and a strong west wind! Sufficient to say that after three full weeks of perfect weather, the Harvest Thanksgiving took place. My nearest neighbour, a typically taciturn Aberdeen-shire farmer, greeted me at the end of the service with a shy smile and the simple comment, 'Someone seems to have heard you!' God's name had been honoured. Later that day I recalled Elijah's prayer: 'O LORD, let it be known that … I am your servant …' (1 Kings 18:36).

My second congregation was in Stirling-shire. The church building was an A-listed Georgian structure dating back to 1820. But it needed restoration of parts of the roof as well as renewal of the original cast-iron gutters and down-pipes. There was also considerable work needed in order to restore the stonework. However, the department in the Scottish Office responsible for listed buildings refused permission for us to proceed. In spite of our pleas, their answer was an emphatic no. An enthusiastic response by both congregation and community had rapidly raised the equivalent today of some £150,000. So what now?

I invited to an elder's home about five members whom I thought would be willing to pray. It was early in that ministry and I doubted if there would have been any others willing to join us, though the congregation totalled well over (on paper) fourteen hundred communicants. After reading from the Scriptures, together we knelt down and cried out to God.

Within two weeks the Scottish Office authorized us to proceed. The architect in charge of the work commented, 'You must have a friend high up in the government to have brought about this reversal.' To this day I regret I did not reply, 'My "Friend" is even higher up than that.' But those who gathered for worship on the Lord's Day were all coming to know that God was that 'Friend'.

The third example of answered prayer concerned a congregation in Ireland where I also ministered. There we had a major two-phase building project planned. First, after nearly one hundred years since the building was opened, they wanted to complete the original plans for the sanctuary; second, they needed to extend the church hall accommodation to more than three times its existing capacity.

Powerful voices in the congregation strongly felt that the first priority was to complete the sanctuary with a major extension. But another very vocal faction felt the urgent need was to provide facilities for the growing children's and youth work. Because we failed to persuade either side to agree on which phase should come first, it was decided to tackle both phases together. The cost was going to be enormous, over five times more than our total annual income.

For several nights I hardly slept. I felt that the decision had been ill-considered. If the project stalled the blame would fall unjustly on myself. More, if we ended up having to borrow half a million pounds, bank interest would significantly increase the cost. So for nearly seventy-two hours I agonized before the Lord.

About 4 am during the third sleepless night God spoke to me: 'The gold and silver are mine and the cattle on a thousand hills. Half a million pounds is nothing to me. Trust me!' Immediately my peace and confidence in the Lord was restored. Thanking him, I fell into a deep sleep.

Shortly after we began the project, we received from a most unexpected source a legacy of just over half a million pounds, and while we used that money in the interim as a loan to pay for the project, in the subsequent years we invested the entire legacy in the Lord's work in other places, retaining nothing for ourselves. It was one of the most remarkable and dramatic answers to earnest prayer that I have ever known.

Dayspring Macleod

Dayspring MacLeod grew up in the United States and moved to Scotland to study literature. She is now privileged to live with her husband in one of the world's most beautiful cities – Edinburgh! Dayspring enjoys theatre, writing, and travel, and worships in the Free Church of Scotland. Read on to find out why this writer has entitled her article: Emmeline.

The date I picked to move to Scotland was 13th September, 2001.

I was seventeen years old, moving from a placid little Ohio town to St Andrews for a year studying abroad. My parents, sending their youngest 3,500 miles away, were as nervous as I was. But we were all excited, too, to see what the future might bring. We had prayed about this decision, and I had felt a leading to the town since I first heard of it.

And then, one bright morning, the Towers fell. Two days before I was to leave, my mother woke me to come and see the news. Like the rest of the nation and the world, we spent the day in front of the TV, stunned. Like much of my generation, I felt a fear that day that I could not have imagined before. The South Tower, the North Tower, the Pentagon, the field in Pennsylvania – it seemed like the atrocities that day would never end, and if they did, they would just start again the minute air traffic resumed.

Throughout the next few days I talked to the godliest people I knew. I prayed and asked them to pray for me. With the air chaos – nobody knew which flights were going, or when – my parents and I ended up making three long, emotional drives to the Detroit airport. Finally, three days after my original booking, I was actually given a seat, and I hugged my parents goodbye. They told me, 'If anything doesn't seem right or feel right about the plane, don't get on.' That possibility frightened me even more, and I broke down in the departure lounge, to be petted back into some semblance of calmness by a female passenger with broken English.

Ah, the good Lord had his angels around me that day. It was a matter of praying without ceasing – for control over my fear and grief, for the safety of my flights, for my parents, for the Lord's presence and comfort, for His help in getting to my new home.

Sometimes we don't know how to pray. If there was a time I groaned in the Spirit, that was surely it. But we usually don't expect the Lord to answer in a very literal way. Yes, I knew that He was with me. I travelled with my Bible and read Psalms as we prepared to take off. I must have had faith that the plane would stay in the air, or I wouldn't have gotten on it. I was nervous about getting to my second flight and finding the correct transportation in Edinburgh; but I would make it somehow. Lord, help me.

In this case, the Lord answered my prayer in a very literal, almost miraculous, sense: He sent me an escort. The girl two seats away from me on the plane was also going to St Andrews. She had already spent a year or two there, and would be beside me all the way to the town. Her name was Emmeline. She told me about St Andrews; in Amsterdam she noticed I didn't have the right boarding pass, and helped me get a new one printed; she got me on to the Edinburgh plane and, once we landed, led me to the student representatives who had come to meet us.

I never saw Emmeline again. This seemed odd to me in a town of 25,000 people where one ran into the same faces day after day. I often wondered whether she was an angel the Lord had sent to comfort and help me. More likely she was just a fellow student whom He used. All that really matters is that, just as the Great Jehovah provided manna in the wilderness or wine for a wedding feast, for me He provided Emmeline. She was not only a guide in time of need, she was also a confirmation that I was doing the right thing in coming to St Andrews and not giving up on my plan.

It is often in the times when my heart has been breaking with need and worry that I have seen the Lord work in extraordinary ways. In times when my faith has been running low and I have stopped believing He will provide, I have still not stopped praying for His provision. And the Lord sometimes brings us to that point, I believe, quite deliberately. We could not give Him the glory He is due without first going through the suffering and knowing His wondrous deliverance.

The child must know its helplessness and throw itself on the Father. How else are we to learn faith and perseverance, but through the Father showing His intervening grace when all seems lost? 'Why did you doubt?' Jesus asks Peter after he sinks into the sea; I have felt Him ask me the same gentle question. And I have found that when He sends His overwhelming blessings, I can do nothing but return thanks, and then, knowing my own lack of resources, open my hands and ask for yet more. *I lift my eyes to the hills – where does my help come from?*

In the Old Testament, the nation of Israel is constantly remembering their exodus from Egypt, and the Lord's amazing deliverance from their slavery as they passed through the Red Sea. I don't have space here to tell of the Lord's last-minute provisions of the piano or house I needed, His help with permanent immigration which unexpectedly also led me to my husband, His guidance when I was deciding what to do after university, or His gracious sense of grace and wooing when I was struggling with assurance. Just as He delivered me from fear that terrible week after 9/11, His greatest gift to us all is our deliverance from the bondage of sin and fear through the sacrifice of His Son, the Lamb.

What times in your own life do you remember and marvel at the Lord's answer to your prayers?

Dorothy Patterson

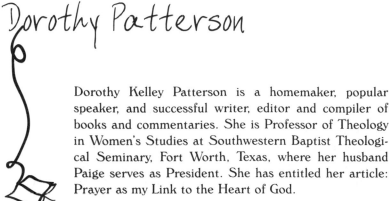

Dorothy Kelley Patterson is a homemaker, popular speaker, and successful writer, editor and compiler of books and commentaries. She is Professor of Theology in Women's Studies at Southwestern Baptist Theological Seminary, Fort Worth, Texas, where her husband Paige serves as President. She has entitled her article: Prayer as my Link to the Heart of God.

Nothing is more important to the Lord God than your personal relationship to Him. God opens the door for you as His child to have a personal and intimate relationship with Him through prayer. Not only do you affirm His promise to meet your needs and empower you to do His work, but you also express a poignant awareness of your dependence upon Him in all of life.

Although in prayer a myriad of earthly blessings join with heavenly purposes, several reasons come to mind concerning why prayer is important to me personally.

My heart overflows with adoration and praise as well as thanksgiving for what the Lord has done in my own personal life. I read through the book of Psalms each month (five chapters a day). In a devotional reading from Psalms 40–45, as I read the marginal notes made with my pen in earlier readings of Psalm 40:5, I was reminded that I rejoiced in 2010, using the words of this Psalm when the Lord answered my petition for a matching gift to complete the funding of Southwestern Seminary's new chapel. I was in London praying earnestly, and the Lord placed the name of a dear friend and kingdom supporter in my heart during my prayer time. I called him, and he immediately responded to meet the need. The very same verse was in my devotional reading later in 2010 when God answered my prayer to provide the remaining funds for our Southwestern Seminary Dead Sea Scroll acquisition! Yes, He does meet needs and answer our petitions; and prayer is the tool for responding to that provision with a heart of gratitude.

When you know in your heart that you have failed spiritually, whether uttering a careless word or failing to give a witness to the gospel or allowing an attitude of anger or bitterness to grip you, you can use prayer to go directly to the Father and ask His forgiveness and restoration. You can have your joy in the Lord restored even as King David expressed (Ps. 51:10-12). When you experience frustration and hurt, you can pour out your feelings to the Lord—for His ears only—and be washed and cleansed and revived. I remember vividly when my husband was unjustly treated by a ministry, experiencing public humiliation and hurt. His name was as quickly cleared as it was besmirched, but the pain to our family and the wasted time of walking through that deep valley are still memories. Yet through it all, God was faithful! We had a front-row seat to watch how He worked His good for us and gave us so much more than we could have ever dreamed (Rom. 8:28)!

Through prayer you can make life-changing decisions! I have found careful and wise guidance in my life journey (Matt. 6:33). How well I remember just on the eve of entering my sixth decade and in the midst of overwhelming success in the ministry God had given to my husband and me in North Carolina, God again clearly and firmly called us to a new and greater challenge in Texas. Humanly it was unwise and even potentially hurtful to us. Seemingly our chance 'to finish well' could be ruined. I pleaded with the Lord to let that cup pass and let us continue serving Him in full strength and completing what we had begun. However, the Lord said "no" to my request and made clear that we must leave the security and joy of what was going well and venture again into the unknown. So we did, and we have had not only overwhelming challenges but also the greatest rewards of our entire ministry years. He has indeed shown His faithfulness (Isa. 43:1-3).

Finally, prayer provides a venue for fellowship with other believers. I cherish my prayer partners in the gospel. My staff and I come together each week for planning. Always the first thing on our agenda is to share requests around the table and then to take these requests before the Lord—sometimes with many tears but always with united hearts and inevitably with power that comes in such corporate prayer (Matt. 18:20). The prayer force behind Southwestern Seminary is primarily a group called *Widows Might*. These women receive prayer requests from the seminary on a regular basis—via telephone, email, letters, or in our retreats. They take the responsibility of praying very seriously. That means the power of heaven called down for this work God has given us to do, but it also means a bonding of sisters to do the work of the kingdom. Their fellowship not only gives strength to the work of the Lord, but it also encourages them individually and enables them to serve the Lord effectively, offering blessings along the way. Even if they cannot leave their own homes, they are part of an extraordinary fellowship laboring in the kingdom vineyard.

God uses your conversation with Him in prayer to respond to you. He may answer, *yes, no,* or *wait*; but He always answers. Your comfort will come in laying all your burdens before Him. Through the relationship you build with Him by this intimate communication, you will learn that He alone sees the beginning and ending of your life, and He knows how your petitions fit into His perfect purposes for your life. Because He is good, whatever the challenges that come your way, He goes before you, walks with you, and is your rearguard. He allows you to glorify Him even in difficulty and suffering, but He never leaves you alone in the journey. Even if you are too weary and distraught to know how to pray, He comes alongside to help you voice your needs (Rom. 8:26).

Esther Harding

Esther Harding was born and raised in the U.S.A. and born into God's family as a fourteen-year-old. When she married her British husband in 2006 she moved to the U.K. and is now a home-schooling wife and mother with two young girls. She enjoys baking, reading, and volunteering with United Beach Missions. She has entitled her article: Learning to Pray.

I grew up with the blessings of a Biblical church and godly, first-generation Christian parents. I am so thankful for the strong foundation that this gave my life. However, having a strong foundation did not mean that I understood or implemented what I had been taught. Much of this teaching fell on the deaf ears of one whose heart had not yet been changed by God. This foundational teaching would have been worthless if God had not used it to call me to salvation through Jesus' life sacrifice. It is because I can approach God in prayer that I have even been saved!

Prayer is my life-line to God. It directly impacts my relationship with Him. I cannot grow in my relationship with Him unless I spend time with Him in Bible reading, hiding His Word in my heart, and in prayer. When I pray, I worship and thank God for all His abundant goodness to me, I confess my sin and ask for His Holy Spirit for help in pleasing God, and I bring all my needs to God, my Father.

I feel greatly inadequate to write anything on prayer; my prayer life is so weak. I thank God that He is instructing me, and growing me in this area. Until relatively recently, I had felt keenly that I had almost no idea how to pray, despite my Christian upbringing. I need to learn about prayer.

I am learning that praying simply is okay. I had long thought my prayers needed to be like other people's prayers. It seemed to me that the public prayers I heard were grand and lofty. Sometimes I would lose the plot while listening to prayers because they were complicated. As I grew older, I started to notice other prayers; prayers that were simple, Biblical, and earnest. They were more like my own simple, matter-of-fact, and feeble, but believing prayers. I started to think that maybe I could pray 'right'. Although I can now appreciate and follow eloquent prayers and I know that they have their place, I also know that Christ hears the simplest of prayers and the unspoken yearnings of our hearts. The prayer Jesus taught His disciples was simple (Matt. 6:9-13) and we are told the Holy Spirit intercedes for believers when we don't know how to form our prayers (Rom. 8:26).

I am learning that prayer should come naturally and be constant. The people I think have most impacted my prayer life are a family I met when I was living in Scotland. They are just an ordinary family without a strong Christian upbringing, but their prayer life seems to be beyond my own. To them, prayer seems as natural as breathing and eating, or as easy as talking to best friends. They say they pray for us and we know they really do. When we were together, they made a point of praying with us. When confronted with a problem, they cast their cares on God by stopping to pray then and there. They live out the biblical command to pray without ceasing (1 Thess. 5:17).

Another thing that teaches me to pray constantly is my need. It is intense, hard work being a mom of two toddlers with a husband who travels for work. In my day-to-day life there are frequent temptations to be short-suffering, not long-suffering. I need help! The Lord is teaching me to rely on His strength. When I need patience, He is ready to aid me in obeying Him. When I need strength, He surprises me by granting me more than I expected. When I need comfort or someone to talk to, God is glorified by me casting my burdens on Him! I pray to Him in the moment as things are happening, by stopping everything to pray with a child, or by calling out to Him for patience in a situation because mine is insufficient. How thankful I am that He is always there and I, as His blood-bought child, can pray to Him where I am and as I am.

I am learning to make time for prayer. I rarely find time to have prayer 'dates' (or do I not make the time?). Daniel did so three times a day (Dan. 6:10). God is the most important person in my life, so I should yearn for special times set aside for Him and me alone. That is something I know I need, but rarely accomplish. When I do have special prayer times, I find that I can get carried away talking with, or pouring my heart out to God. These are precious times, like catching up with an old friend.

I am learning that spiritual wellbeing is more important than physical wellbeing. This is apparent from Scripture. Christ prayed, 'I do not pray that You should take them [my disciples] out of the world, but that You should keep them from the evil one' (John 17:15; see also Matt. 6:25,32 NKJV). He certainly cares for our physical needs (see Matt. 6:11,25,32), but our spiritual life is far more important. This is what will last forever. I need to learn to pray more for spiritual needs (such as contentment) instead of physical needs (e.g. the resolution to hubby's on-going job issue).

As I learn all these things, my relationship with God grows. God cares for me so much that He sacrificed His most precious thing for me: His Son. How much more will He provide everything I need? (Rom. 8:32) Even though life can be difficult and confusing, when I am with God after death I will not doubt His love because I will fully appreciate that He heard all my prayers. He is answering them all, whether 'yes' or 'no', for His glory and my eternal good.

Heather Holdsworth

Heather and her husband, Adrian, serve at The Faith Mission Bible College, Edinburgh. She lectures in Spiritual Formation and Children and Youth Ministry and is passionate about stirring up honest worshippers. To relax there's canoeing and painting – not in combo! She has entitled her article: Thoughts on Prayer – for New and Used Believers.

How do you know when someone is a true disciple, a wholehearted follower? With what do you gauge commitment? In our evangelical hamlets, measurements are constantly taken. And most often, the unit by which we log devotion is activity.

With each morning, demands roll in. Flurries of tasks squeeze the stopwatch and the ticking begins. Sixteen hours of useable minutes and so much to do. The countdown arrives unbidden, before one page of Scripture sees daylight.

Focus.

Open eyes.

Open Bible.

Each minute puts pressure on the text for results, to find some bright phrase to align our day. With the reading over, comes the puzzle of prayer. It seems a call to inaction.

'Be still'.

'Wait'.

'Abide'.

The instructed pause on our lives of purpose; can we seriously afford the time?

So prayer becomes a briefing; where we roll out events; highlight areas of responsibility. We notify the Christ to pour smoothness on this day – emotional cheer, financial calm and easy parking – the evidences of God's sanction on our activities.

We move out and the action starts. Is our soul still? Did we 'abide'? If there was time for an honest moment, we sit closer to guilt than satisfaction. But hey, many Christians don't even have devotions – read any survey.

And what about when the sun doesn't shine for the kids' Bible Club and the bank balance shade is more red than black? When the doctor pauses too long before giving those results and your mum's forgetfulness triggers family e-mails? When God didn't follow the script you covered in the morning memo – what then?

Do you just stand and sing heartily so that the words from your lips are louder than the questions of your heart?

Do you leave God at the planning meeting with clear objectives – to bless the lists; to make guest appearances at special meetings? But that isn't a relationship. Not in anyone's book.

So how do we find relational contentment with an unseen God? Jesus' frequent method of engaging people was parables; obscure stories relying wholly on two things for meaning – a teacher and his insight. As the disciples pursued Jesus away from the crowds on the beach to pathways and homes, something happened. Doubt and unwashed faith trumped any urge to be seen, any need to sound right. Frank dialogues with the Saviour in unplanned places were what changed perceptions, rocketed growth, and made them come alive!

I am done with confining God to small spaces, with segregating him to a convenient zone while I hold sway over the activities of life. I am finished with treating him as capable only to deal with the tasks assigned. I'm done with the divide between 'devotions' and devotion. It's as smart as trying to split body from breath. If this relationship works, it has to work in every situation and every space.

A friend asked some years back whether I struggled with prayer. 'Yes, I do' was my reply.

My husband looked over at me, puzzled, 'Heather, you talk to God all the time.'

'Well yes, I talk to him all the time, but I struggle with prayer'; that earnest staging of correct theology. There was quiet and then the question, 'And what is it you teach kids that prayer is?'

My automatic response, 'Well, prayer is ... ah. Yes!'

But how is this workable? Lengthening our devotional practices? There are so many pressures, we honestly don't have the time. No, I am not speaking of more obligations – here is the gold.

Reactions

Throughout each day we experience life and react. Each news headline provokes a response. What if God was actively invited into the way we process life? What if information was handled with him? What if the photo from a bomb blast began a different sentence, 'Lord, you see that lady, this child. You hear their agony. I'm listening – how do you want me to pray?'

And when a car passes with a fish on its window, pray strength for his faith and hope for his family.

And at night time when those news stories of terror have fuelled imaginations of attack? Process the thought with the one who has power. Engage. 'Lord, this fear is not my reality right now. But somewhere it is true of one of your disciples. Send angels; bring help; confound her attackers ...' For a long time I prayed daily for the persecuted church. And the enemy of souls realised that his plan of paralysing me through fear was backfiring badly. And he moved on to another scheme.

Triggers

Each day you do things the same as the last. Your teeth need brushing, shoes need to be put on and your desk lamp needs to shine. I use daily things to prompt me to pray for people. For Julie and Erin when I brush my teeth, for Viktor as I switch on his old desk lamp and each night as I switch off the bedside light a little luminous star shines from the shade! That tiny glow triggers a chain. I begin by praying for a friend 4000 miles away and later when her star shines, she prays for me. And then I swim out, deep and far into the oceanic current of

God's mercy and WORSHIP my Saviour who has gone beyond being recognised and charted to being my utter delight!

Inviting God into your living means you track together all day. And he leads and he speaks and your sight is shaped by his heart. It's a life-giving conversation. Eyes open, ears wide, an active participant in life with the Master of it.

Heather Thompson

Heather Thompson trained and served as a Hotel Manager in Great Britain for a national chain before getting married to Ian in 1985. They have three great kids. She now lives with her husband and daughter in Bethlehem, Pennsylvania, U.S.A. She has entitled her article: What does Prayer Mean to Me?

Prayer is that part of my life that makes me feel alive. When I am talking to my Heavenly Father I know that he is listening. Can he listen to all our prayers and be personally interested in all of us? YES! That is amazing because there are days when I talk to him a lot.

Those days are when I have deep concerns on my heart, or friends are having a hard time, or when I have things to do that I find hard and I want to bring glory to him.

I pray over my cooking—especially when I am making a new recipe or baking cookies for a special occasion.

I pray over my vegetable garden—when I am weeding I think about all the sins in my life that keep coming back, just like weeds, and I need to ask God to forgive me. I pray over my newly planted trees—I want them to grow strong and to be a pleasure to sit under. I pray over my flowers—that they will be a pleasure to look at. The plants grow in secret and so does my prayer life.

When I think about prayer I look at Jesus and see how often he prayed. It was so important to him that his disciples wanted to learn how to pray like he did—so he taught them the Lord's Prayer as a pattern.

At school, I went to assembly where I learnt and said the Lord's Prayer every school day for twelve years. Prayers were always part of the church service on a Sunday, recited from a prayer book. I knew that I could speak to God, but felt that he must be tired of hearing the same prayers over and over again.

But about five years after I left school I found out that I could REALLY pray and talk to God and that he listens and answers me. He had adopted me, I had become a Christian, and it's only his adopted children who can talk to him and call him by the familiar name of Abba (Papa).

YES! I have been turned the right way up in the center of my life by Jesus and I know God as my Father through faith in his Son. That's why I can pray to my Father in heaven, and know he is listening. Even when Jesus prayed to God, he used the word Father—that is amazing!

When I think about this I am humbled because God, who made everything, knows everything and knows everyone, hears me and knows me. I am invited to talk to God, actually invited into his throne room. I don't think I will ever be invited to speak to a president, king, or prime minister, yet at any time I am able to speak to God without an appointment. There is no waiting and wondering if he is going to allow me to speak to him. He actually delights in my talking to him.

Prayer isn't always easy though, I may think I know what I should do in a situation, but when I truly seek God he has much better answers to my prayers. He sees everything and knows everything so, his way is the best way.

How can I know him better and know his will better? I need to continue to read the Bible and to grow in my prayer life, because if I don't know God, how can I pray to him as a person?

Dear God, Thank you for always being there for your children. Thank you that we can come to you and know you hear us. Thank you that you are in heaven and one day I will be there with you. Lord, thank you that I can think about heaven and when I do, things that are bothering me here on earth seem to grow less important. Please forgive my sins and all that I think and do that are wrong, through Jesus Christ, my Saviour, Amen.

Ishbel Murray

Ishbel Murray is wife to Craig and mother to Katrin, Robbie and Elspeth. She lives and works as a nurse in Fort William, Scotland. She was brought up by Christian parents and has fond memories of Christian grandparents too. Ishbel loves being involved in her local church and seeing God making a real impact on people's lives.

When I was asked to write a chapter on prayer I thought what *does* prayer mean to me? Over the years I have read many books and heard many a talk on prayer. I've heard about the ACTS (acknowledge, confess, thanksgiving and supplication) way of praying, the teaspoon prayer TSP (thanks, sorry, please) even the toast prayer (totally awesome, others, ask, sorry, thanks). I've read books on being too busy not to pray, housewives' adventures with prayer, I've been enthralled and sometimes bored by other people's prayers. Indeed as a child some prayers felt like an endurance event! The best advice on prayer is obviously from Scripture but one of the best ways I learnt about prayer was through examples of godly men and women I have loved and respected through the years.

My paternal grandmother, Dolly MacKenzie, was an example to me in prayer. In a day and church where public prayer by women was never heard we were very privileged to hear her pray when she babysat. She always opened her prayer with the words 'Darling Jesus'. To hear her pray like that was a revelation. I thought that it was curious but profoundly moving that she was able to address Jesus in that way and it became apparent that I did not think of Jesus as my darling. I realised that she must have a very personal, close and loving relationship with him to be able to call him darling.

My maternal grandfather, Willie MacKenzie, is another wonderful example. He always commenced his public prayers with the phrase 'Oh most holy and ever blessed one'. The tone of voice and the words gave a sense of reverence, a sense of awe and wonder that such an almighty God was listening to us, a very humbling prospect.

My father and mother, Hugh and Mary MacKenzie, also taught my brothers and myself to start our prayers 'Lord bless us and teach us to pray' which is a biblical principal found in Luke chapter 11. The disciples asked Jesus, 'Lord teach us to pray,' which led to Jesus teaching the disciples the Lord's Prayer.

Using the Bible to help us pray is a concept I should have used long before I did. While with the Operation Mobilisation summer scheme 'Love Europe' I learnt to take a passage of Scripture and work through it line by line, praying through it, meditating on it and applying it. The Bible tells us so much about prayer and gives us great examples of prayer such as Hannah's prayer in 1 Samuel and Jonah's prayer in the first chapter of Jonah. In the New Testament we find Jesus praying for us in the Gospels and in 1 Thessalonians chapter 5 the apostle Paul also speaks about praying without ceasing which as a child was a very strange concept to me. How can anybody pray all day every day? That just didn't make sense. But as I have gone on with the Lord I think it means turning the mundane things to him as well as the big things. As you are tempted to shout at someone when they cut you up on the road, pray for them instead and thank God that he has kept you safe on life's journey thus far. When you pass sad people on the street or happy children in a playground ask that the Lord would reveal himself to them.

Other practical ways to help with praying that have been demonstrated to me and I have used over the years have been to use a prayer diary or journal. It's a great way of reminding myself, should I need reminding, of how God does answer prayer from the big stuff to the little stuff of life. Praying with a list in front of you is an aid to concentration. It is that lack of concentration that I find one of the biggest obstacles to prayer. How many times do we find that the phone will ring or the postie will knock on the door or something will happen to affect your concentration as you try to pray? Or if you're like me somebody's name or a situation that needs prayer will trigger another random but connected thought and then that thought will lead to another and so on. That is where I find that a list in front of you or indeed writing your prayers is useful. At times when concentration is at a low ebb speaking your prayers out loud can really help.

Prayer is talking to God and it is about employing your mind while doing so. One of my favourite Colin Buchanan songs says you've got to:

Take every thought and catch it, gotcha
Chuck out all of that sin, bye bye
Take every thought and catch it
and think about J-E-S-U-S
Fix your thoughts on him.

(Quoted from *Take Every Thought and Catch it* by Colin Buchanan Copyright Universal Music Publishing (Aust). Reprinted by permission).

The Holy Spirit

Likewise the Spirit helps us in our weakness. For we do not know what to pray for as we ought, but the Spirit himself intercedes for us with groanings too deep for words (Rom. 8:26 ESV).

Jessie McFarlane

Jessie McFarlane is the founder of Prayer Chain Ministries, a women's telephone prayer system and the author of *A Housewife's Adventure with God*. She has entitled this article: The Cinderella of the Church!

I became a follower of Jesus Christ when I was eleven years old. I was told to read my Bible, go to Church and pray. I enjoyed reading my Bible and going to Church was great, but I found praying a problem; not so much when I was a child, but as I grew older it seemed my prayers reached no higher than the ceiling. God seemed distant. I was a wife and mother of four children and when things were going well prayer was put on the back burner, but when problems appeared I was on my knees expecting God to get me out of them. God's amazing grace upheld me through many of these difficulties!

As I grew older, I realised something was missing in my Christian life. I attended Church every Sunday, I was even busy singing around Glasgow and a wider area, but something was unreal. One evening when I was singing at a meeting an old lady came to me afterwards, shook me by the hand and said, 'I can see that's real to you.' The hymn I had sung was:

> All my days and all my hours,
> All my will and all my powers.
> All the passion of my soul

Not a fragment but the whole,
Shall be Thine O Lord.

This was not real to me. God did not have all my days and all my hours, nor did He have the passion of my soul. When I got home, I got down on my knees and asked God to 'make me real'.

This began a process of God answering my prayer, but had I known how He would answer, I may not have prayed. I started studying what the Bible says about prayer and reading books on prayer and I became aware that when I prayed I came into the presence of the Holy, Holy, Holy God of the Universe and if I expected God to answer my prayers I must meet His requirement of holiness. He commands, 'Be holy, because I am holy' (1 Pet. 1:16 NIV). Holiness is the fundamental attribute of God and His requirement for us. It says in Ephesians 1:4 NIV, 'He chose us in Him before the creation of the world to be holy and blameless in His sight.' That is God's requirement for me and anything less in my life is sin. I also learned that 'if I had cherished sin in my heart the Lord would not have listened' (Ps. 66:18 NIV).

As I endeavoured by God's grace to fulfil the prerequisites for prayer, I became excited at how God opened doors of opportunity to extend His kingdom and encourage others to pray.

Prayer is the power-house of our Christian lives. Perhaps we do not see God's power released in our churches because prayer has become the missing dynamic and is now the Cinderella? This is what the Rev Richard Bewes says about prayer in his book, *150 Pocket Thoughts*. A tingling sense of expectancy characterizes the Church that prays. Church worship, fellowship and outreach become irradiated with the presence and power of Christ Himself when prayer is recognized as the most important activity of all!

We talk about prayer and read about prayer, but when we come to pray together at our church prayer meetings, we often do not come to meet the Living God of the Universe, but to meet each other. We do not expect to receive the power of the Holy Spirit to come down as He did at Pentecost. We pray with no vision of the lost or how we can reach them. Samuel

Chadwick says, 'The world will never believe in a religion in which there is no power.' A rationalised faith, a socialised church, a moralised gospel may gain applause but they awaken no conviction and gain no converts.

Prayer is the most exciting discipline of my Christian life, and I would encourage every young Christian to get into the business of getting to know God through prayer early in their Christian lives.

In the King's Hands

Lord Bolingbroke said to the Countess of Huntingdon, "I cannot understand, Your Ladyship, how you can make out earnest prayer to be consistent with submission to the Divine will."

"My Lord," she said, "that is a matter of no difficulty. If I were a courtier of some generous king and he gave me permission to ask any favour I pleased of him, I should be sure to put it thus, 'Will Your Majesty be graciously pleased to grant me such-and-such a favour—but at the same time, though I very much desire it, if it would in any way detract from Your Majesty's honour, or if in Your Majesty's judgment it should seem better that I did not have this favour, I shall be quite as content to go without it as to receive it.' So you see I might earnestly offer a petition and yet I might submissively leave it in the king's hands."

So with God. We never offer up prayer without inserting that clause, either in spirit or in words, "Nevertheless, not as I will, but as You will. Not my will but Yours be done."

Charles Spurgeon,
Sermon: The Golden Key of Prayer

Joanna Black

Joanna Black was born in Ayrshire, Scotland, and had the great privilege of being brought up in a loving home with her parents, older sister and several pets! Joanna is now working as a Speech and Language Therapist in Glasgow and also works casually at her local theatre. She has many interests, so many in fact, were she to write them down it would take several pages!

How has prayer impacted my life? As I lie awake contemplating this question, thinking about the number of times in my life I've prayed or have been prayed for; recalling the words of specific prayers at significant moments in my life, the conclusion I'm drawn to is simply this: the impact of prayer upon me is immense.

Much of my work as a Speech and Language Therapist is based around the question of impact: what effect does the speech or language impairment, stammer, or voice disorder, have on the person? What does it prevent them from doing? How does it affect their relationships? With this in mind, I've thought about the impact of prayer upon my life.

What effect does prayer have on me? Prayer changes my perspective. It lifts me out of the day to day, worldly grind and into the holy presence of the living God. It focuses my thoughts on Him – my Creator, my Lord and Saviour, my Heavenly Father. It has a humbling effect on me: when I pray, I'm talking to the God who created 'the heavens and the earth in all its vast array'; who made the light and put the stars in place; who 'created my inmost being' – who spoke and it was done (Gen. 1, 2:1 and Ps. 139:13). When I really stop to think about this, I can hardly take it in! I'm talking to the God who loves me so much that he sacrificed his perfect, sinless Son; who bore the inconceivable punishment for my sin, who took my place on the cross, so that I may go free, forgiven, made right with God. Prayer is a daily reminder that God is on the throne; he is Sovereign. Prayer builds me up. How often I lack confidence; but prayer so wonderfully enables me to boldly approach the throne of grace (Heb. 4:16) and talk to God. Prayer has a calming effect on me – I'm reminded that God alone is in control, 'even the wind and the waves obey Him!' (Matt. 8:26-27). I don't need to do it on my own, for 'my help comes from the LORD, the Maker of heaven and earth' (Ps. 121:2 NIV).

What does prayer prevent me from doing? Prayer prevents me from being crushed by the heavy burdens of earthly life. I need not carry the weight of my sin around with me day by day. I can confess it to the Lord in prayer and in his loving grace and mercy, he forgives me and relieves me of this weight. Prayer prevents me from being swallowed up by anxiety or sorrow – I can cast all my cares upon the Lord as He commands me to (Matt. 11:28), knowing that he will sustain me and will never let me fall (Ps. 55:22). I could not count all the times I've taken him at his word, all the times I've taken it to the Lord in prayer. Before – and during – the writing of this piece, I prayed. When I was preparing to sit exams, I prayed. When I was unemployed for long periods of time, I prayed. When I went to live in an unfamiliar city, feeling like a stranger in a foreign land, I prayed. When fear and panic seemed to overcome me, I prayed. When I didn't know what to do, when I didn't understand, when I felt, 'I just can't do it, Lord!', I cried to the Lord in prayer. When I looked on, troubled and frustrated, powerless to stop the suffering of loved ones, I bowed before God and I prayed, and prayed. On the death of precious members of my family, in deepest grief, I drew near to my Heavenly Father in prayer and found the comfort, peace and hope that only He can provide. Oh how I praise the Lord and echo the words of the writer Joseph M. Scriven: 'What a friend we have in Jesus, all our sins and griefs to bear! What a privilege to carry everything to God in prayer!'

How does prayer affect my relationships? Prayer brings me into a close personal relationship with God. I can talk to God about anything, at any time, day or night, for he 'will neither slumber nor sleep' (Ps. 121:4). I communicate to Him my thanks and praise, I confess my sin, I ask for guidance, I bring different people and situations before him, I share my deepest thoughts and feelings – with God I have no secrets. It is a relationship like no other. He always listens. He is never too busy. He has never had enough of me. Oh how often I let him down! He *never* lets *me* down. My prayers never fall on deaf ears (1 Peter 3:12). He will always answer my prayer, even if it's not the answer I've hoped for or expected. God commands obedience in praying without ceasing (1 Thess. 5:17). I don't always find it easy to pray. Sometimes I stumble over the words; sometimes I'm too distracted; sometimes I feel too ashamed of my sin. But I have no excuse for giving up: in his perfect wisdom he has taught me how to pray (Matt. 6:5-15). If I stop praying, I forfeit my close communion with God. What relationship can truly last without regular communication?

Prayer also affects my relationships with other people. In praying with and for God's people, I become united with them in Christ. I become an active member of a very special family – God's family. It is a family that unites in communally praising and glorifying God in prayer. It is a family that is united in providing care and support for each other in prayer. So often I am very aware of the prayers of others for me, for which I am so thankful. A significant part of my prayer life also involves praying for those who do not yet know God as their Saviour: family members, friends, colleagues, people I have only met once or twice, people I have never met, and people who do not know me. Some of these people do not even know that I pray for them, and yet, the very act of bringing them before God in prayer, creates a special bond between us.

Prayer is an extraordinary gift from God; one for which I will be eternally grateful. Prayer impacts my life in ways that I just can't put into words. What would I be like without prayer? What would I do without prayer? Where would I be without prayer? I cannot begin to imagine.

> What a Friend we have in Jesus,
> All our sins and griefs to bear.
> What a privilege to carry,
> Everything to God in prayer.
> O what peace we often forfeit,
> O what needless pain we bear,
> All because we do not carry,
> Everything to God in prayer.
>
> Have we trials and temptations?
> Is there trouble anywhere?
> We should never be discouraged;
> Take it to the Lord in prayer.
> Can we find a friend so faithful,
> Who will all our sorrows share?
> Jesus knows our every weakness;
> Take it to the Lord in prayer.
>
> Are we weak and heavy laden,
> Cumbered with a load of care?
> Precious Saviour, still our refuge,
> Take it to the Lord in prayer.
> Do thy friends despise, forsake thee?
> Take it to the Lord in prayer;
> In his arms he'll take and shield thee,
> Thou wilt find a solace there.
>
> Blessed Saviour, Thou hast promised,
> Thou wilt all our burdens bear.
> May we ever, Lord, be bringing,
> All to Thee in earnest prayer.
> Soon in glory bright unclouded,
> There will be no need for prayer.
> Rapture, praise and endless worship,
> Will be our sweet portion there.

Words by Joseph M. Scriven, 1855

John Ferguson

John Ferguson is the minister of Kingsview Christian Centre (APC) in Inverness. He graduated in 2012 with a PhD in Divinity from the University of Aberdeen.

When I think of prayer, my mind is drawn to Jesus' parable of the persistent widow in Luke 18. She went to the judge, who was unrighteous, and pleaded for justice. Her persistence moved him to act on her behalf and respond to her plea. Jesus tells us that if persistence moves the unrighteous judge then we can be certain it will also move God, who is the righteous judge, to act on our behalf. God will give justice to his elect, who cry to him day and night (Luke 18:7). Justice comes to those who persist in their prayers.

We also learn of the widow's patience in her plea for justice. She patiently followed her course of action until the judge secured justice for her. She did not stray from this path. She did not take justice into her own hands. She did not give up. She did not seek an answer to her plea in any other way. The persistent widow was patient in her plea. Persistence is vitally connected to patience. If we lose patience in prayer then we will not persist much longer. We will then give up on God and search for answers elsewhere that prove dissatisfying. For if we give up on prayer then we give up on the one who knows the secrets of the heart and the only one who is able to fulfil the desires of the heart. We must persist in prayer and be patient in prayer, waiting for God to respond according to his good will.

In my own life I have found that the Lord answers prayer in diverse ways. Sometimes he answers prayers immediately. Other times he will wait before answering. This wait can be very long. Some of my prayers have been answered after a period of years. Other prayers I have prayed for years and am still waiting to learn the Lord's answer. In conversations with other Christians I have discovered that I am not alone in this experience of waiting. I have met many who have similar experiences in prayer. Indeed I have met men and women who have brought particular requests before God for many years, even decades, and are staying on that course of persistence and patience, as they wait upon the Lord to answer them. If you have waited many years for an answer to your prayer, it is helpful to know that others share in that experience too. Perhaps you have not yet started, or recently began the path of persistence and patience in prayer. You may have to wait a long time before knowing the answers to your prayers, but it is always worth the wait. For it is the testimony of God's people that none who wait for the Lord shall be put to shame (Ps. 25:3).

The answers which I have had to wait the longest for have concerned things that are personally very important to me, including work, marriage and the salvation of friends who are not yet Christians. When personal prayers go unanswered for a long time we may doubt and question. Is it right to say the same prayers after many years? Does God hear me? Does prayer work? These thoughts have crossed my mind as I've waited for answers. We need to be reminded that the story of the persistent widow is a parable of Jesus—a story which he uses to teach us about our relationship with God and therefore how we ought to approach God. Jesus tells us to persist in our prayers and to be patient in our course as we wait for God's answers. He knows better than anyone, for God heard his voice (Heb. 5:7). His voice was heard because he patiently lived in obedience to his Father. The parable teaches that it is God's desire for us to persist and be patient. In this we are reminded that he is God, that it is his will which is done and in his own time. It is right then that we may have to wait a long time before we know the answers to our prayers.

You may, like me, have prayers and you long to see the day when they are answered. If we are waiting and finding it hard to persist and be patient, we can find encouragement from what Jesus says following the parable of the persistent widow. He teaches that God answers the prayers of his people for justice (v. 7) with the second coming of his Son (v.8). Jesus is therefore drawing our attention to prayer for his second coming. This prayer has been offered to God not only for years, but for generations since Christ's first coming. God has not yet sent his Son for the second time and so we join the generations by persisting in this prayer and waiting patiently for God to answer it. So we must learn this same way for all our prayers—whether we are beginning to pray or have been praying for many years.

The Lord is at Hand

Rejoice in the Lord always; again I will say, rejoice. Let your reasonableness be known to everyone. The Lord is at hand; do not be anxious about anything, but in everything by prayer and supplication with thanksgiving let your requests be made known to God. And the peace of God, which surpasses all understanding, will guard your hearts and your minds in Christ Jesus (Phil. 4:4-7 ESV).

John Piper

John Piper is the founder and teacher of desiringGod. org, chancellor of Bethlehem College and Seminary, and author of over fifty books. For thirty-two years, he served as pastor of Bethlehem Baptist Church, Minneapolis, Minnesota (USA). John and his wife Noël have four children and twelve grandchildren.

God delights in the prayers of the upright for the same reason that he abominates the sacrifices of the wicked – because the prayers of the upright are the extension and outworking of the heart; but, unlike the heart of the wicked, the heart of the upright magnifies the power and grace of God. The prayer of the upright is a delight to God because it expresses those affections of the heart which call attention to the all-sufficiency of God.

In Psalm 147:11 we read that "The Lord takes pleasure in those who hope in his love." Here we see that the Lord takes pleasure in prayers that give expression to that hope. The reason our hope is a pleasure to God is because it shows that all our joy comes from the bounty of his grace. And the reason our prayers are a pleasure to God is because they express this God-exalting hope. It is a precious thing beyond all words–especially in the hour of death–that we have a God whose nature is such that what pleases him is not our work for him but our need of him.

The intensity of God's pleasure in prayer becomes more and more obvious as we look at the connection between

prayer and the other things that God is committed to with
all his heart.

For example, God loves to magnify his glory in the lives of
his people. So he designed prayer as a way for this to happen.
Jesus says, "Whatever you ask in my name, I will do it, that the
Father may be glorified in the Son" (John 14:14). So God has
designed prayer as an occasion when he and the Son will be
glorified as the source and agent in doing good to his people.
This is one of the reasons Revelation describes the prayers of
the saints as golden bowls of incense before the throne of God
(Rev. 5:8). God delights in the aroma of his own glory as he
smells it in the prayers of his people.

It is as though God has a favorite food. When we pray, he
smells that aroma from the kitchen as you prepare his special
dish. When God hungers for some special satisfaction, he seeks
out a prayer to answer. Our prayer is the sweet aroma from
the kitchen ascending up into the King's chambers making him
hungry for the meal. But the actual enjoyment of the meal is his
own glorious work in answering our prayer. The food of God
is to answer our prayers. The most wonderful thing about the
Bible is that it reveals a God who satisfies his appetite for joy by
answering prayers. He has no deficiency in himself that he needs
to fill up, so he gets his satisfaction by magnifying the glory of
his riches by filling up the deficiencies of people who pray.

This seems to be the point of Psalm 50:13-15. "Do I eat
the flesh of bulls, or drink the blood of goats?" says the Lord.
No. Therefore "offer to God a sacrifice of thanksgiving ... and
call upon him in the day of trouble, and he will deliver you, and
you shall glorify [him]." The demonstration of the glory of God
in answered prayer is God's special feast. So if we want to feed
him with the only kind of joy he is capable of, we hold up the
empty cup of prayer and let him show the riches of his glory by
filling it. Thus the intensity of God's delight in his glory is the
measure of his pleasure in the prayers of his people.

John van Eyk

In 2008 John van Eyk moved with his wife, Lucy, and their children from Canada to Tain in the Scottish Highlands. He serves an Associated Presbyterian Church congregation there. He has entitled his article: Never Unprayed For.

I f you haven't said it yourself, you've probably thought it. Despite your child's best efforts to prepare the guest room you've thought, "If you want something done right, you've got to do it yourself."

That thought never crosses my mind when I reflect on prayer. I am keenly aware that if my blessing depended on my prayers I would be a very sorry individual. Thankfully, it doesn't. One of the most refreshing things the Bible says about prayer is that the Lord Jesus Christ prays for his people.

Think of Peter. He is rash but you must admire his declaration, "Lord, I am ready to go with you to prison and to death." Even if it sounds self-reliant this is our longing too, isn't it? We wish to go wherever Christ calls us, to follow him whatever the cost.

If we have trouble seeing ourselves in Peter's confident declaration, we have no difficulty finding ourselves in Peter's cowardly denial. But Peter's story doesn't end there. He was restored and became an inestimable blessing to the Church, both in his day and to the present.

What made impetuous Peter the man he was? The same thing that makes us the Christians we are. His usefulness was not by dint of hard work or due to his prevailing prayer; it was because Christ prayed for him.

Before our Lord's arrest, he told Peter that Satan was going to prey on him. Satan was asking to sift Peter as wheat, to subject him to a severe trial. If you have any familiarity with the attacks of the roaring lion you know how unsettling this can be. We are no match for the devil's schemes. No wonder Jesus encouraged his disciples to watch and pray.

But sometimes we don't pray. Perhaps it is because of sickness or tiredness. At other times we are dumb before God because we are overwhelmed by our circumstances and we don't know what or how to pray. We can be so disheartened, we are silent. Occasionally we are prayerless because we are careless. And sometimes we fail to pray because of our own sinfulness: we either think God will not hear our prayers or in rebellion we refuse to pray.

The encouraging truth is that when Christ's disciples do not pray for themselves they are not unprayed for. Satan might prey on Peter, but Jesus assures Peter that he will pray for him. Christ will intercede with the Father on Peter's behalf so that Peter will be restored after Satan has sifted him.

If Christ prayed for Peter why did he fall? Are his prayers ineffective? It is clear that Jesus knew Peter would fall and that Peter would be restored. So why did Peter fall? We cannot presume to comprehend fully the plans and purposes of God but we do know our praying Saviour is always heard by his Father and that his prayers are never denied. He knows the mind of the Father and his desires are the Father's desires. He always prays according to his Father's will.

Peter was restored and he strengthened his brothers. And all because the Lord Jesus prayed for him.

All spiritual life in us is not, in the first place, because of our prayers. Even that we pray at all can be traced back to the Lord Jesus who prays for us. The victorious Conqueror is enthroned at his Father's right hand and prays that his triumph over Satan by his cross would be realised in our lives until the day when faith becomes sight and our enemy is finally destroyed.

May Christ's commitment to intercede for us spur us on to greater prayer for ourselves and others and in our prayers may we thank him for his.

A Mother's Prayer

Hudson Taylor is famous for being a missionary in China and the founder of the China Inland Mission now OMF. But his teenage years were not lived in submission to God. He, in fact, caused great anxiety for his mother who was often in prayer for her rebellious son. On one rather tedious afternoon when his mother was away visiting relatives, Hudson Taylor wandered into his father's library to find something to read. He happened to pick up and read a gospel tract. It was his intention to put the tract down if it got too 'preachy'. However, he could not shake off its message and finally fell to his knees, and accepted Christ as his Saviour. Later, his mother returned to hear Hudson's good news,

To her son's surprise she told him, 'I already know. Ten days ago, the very date on which you tell me you read that tract, I spent the entire afternoon in prayer for you until the Lord assured me that my wayward son had been brought into the fold.'

Katie Maclean

Katie Maclean is a trained nurse and a native of the Isle of Lewis. She now lives in Inverness with her husband who is a Free Church of Scotland minister.

It has never ceased to amaze me that God's ears are always tuned to our hearts and that the Creator of all things is faithful to hear and answer our prayers. I was brought up in a strong Christian community where a previous generation was poor and prayed to God for their most basic needs – like their next meal. As I listened to these stories, what always struck me was their lack of surprise at God's provision. They knew their Heavenly Father well and they had no doubt as to what He was capable of providing. Their God was big. And throughout my own Christian life it has been a wonderful privilege to go to that big God with all my needs and to receive some amazing answers. When problems are unbearable, when things come into our lives that no one on earth understands, what a privilege to talk to someone who wants to talk with us and who has all the answers to our questions and to our needs!

As I reflect on my own prayer life I realise that I often come with my own agenda...well thought out plans waiting for His stamp of approval. But God does not work according to our plans .... He likes to surprise us. We only have to look at all the amazing answers to prayer in the Bible. Who would have thought Sarah would have a child in her nineties? I once read that what is most changed by prayer is the one who is praying. As we spend time with God, things move a little and we are given a new perspective on what we see and what we need.

God is such a God of grace. Even when it seems that He only hears from us when we want something...in His patient love He listens to us.

Hebrews 4:14-16 speaks of the fact that Jesus is praying for us as we pray for others and not only does He pray for us He also prays with us. He is infinitely concerned about us.

I know I should do it more often, give it more time and take it more seriously because prayer is not a kind of 'in case of emergency spiritual tool'... prayer is our path to building a relationship with God. He is aware of all our thoughts, our choices and our movements and He is waiting to hear about it. Undoubtedly the hardest part of prayer is waiting for the answer but I suspect God wants us to go on asking until it is the right time to get an answer.

Kenneth Mackenzie

Kenneth Mackenzie became a widower in December 2011, father of five children and grandfather of thirteen little ones. He enjoys his work as a business man and travels frequently. Kenneth is on the board of several charities, including Wycliffe, Prison Fellowship, and Trinity Forum.

B rought up in a Christian home I was used to family worship. Grace was said before and after all meals, and my mother would even close her eyes and pray quietly before she had a drink of water. So you would think I should have known about prayer. Sure I was used to bending my knee at the side of the bed morning and evening and 'saying my prayers'. But was that really praying?

Then there was the whole procession of my older brothers all publicly professing their faith in the Lord Jesus Christ at various church services over the years,., and finally my father (whom I respected enormously) made a public profession of his faith. This was after years of being fearful of his own assurance of salvation. That meant I was the 'last man standing'.

January 1968 was a challenging period for me, I was diagnosed with TB and admitted to an isolation ward for a month. It was there that I was started on a course of treatment. There was much prayer for me and many godly people visited in order to show their love and compassion. But one prayer stood out and it was not what you might expect.

In the next room, there was an old docker, who worked at the harbour in Inverness. He was a bit of a rogue but he had become a friend. In fact when I think of him now I'm reminded of the character Elisha in Tolstoy's famous story *Two Old Men*: 'He was a kindly and cheerful old man. It is true he drank sometimes, and he took snuff ...'

Anyway one night I was woken by the sound of my friend making strange noises. I got out of my bed and pressed my ear to the glass window between us. The dear man could not speak without swearing, it was just part of his vocabulary. I was used to some of that on the rugby field, playing the sport that was my idol. But as I listened some more I realised that the docker was praying. Yes, bad words were littered throughout his supplications, but he was praying earnestly, for the doctors, the nurses, his own health ... and what was that? Did I hear right? He was praying for his young friend next door ...

When my father came to visit, I was able to send him through to pray with the docker. Father was delighted to do so. He had been chairman of the Inverness Harbour Board Trust, and his company was its major customer importing cement for the emerging green industry ... hydro-electric power. He related well to the humble docker. Ironically he had previously broken a docker strike in Inverness harbour one day by taking off his jacket and loading bags of cement from coastal vessels to the transport waiting on the docks. However, that didn't stop him praying for this earnest old rogue.

In October 1968 I went off to Aberdeen university to do an Arts degree. I stayed in 'digs' the word we used for the student accommodation of the day, I lived there with one of my brothers. Family worship continued in the usual way, but one brother prayed sincerely ...

Exams followed at the end of the university term and my Maths mark was woeful. I had previously received top grades through the whole of my school career ... now 27% was the best I could achieve. I had taken notes poorly in lectures, had missed a significant part of the course due to the TB, and had studied poorly.

I was deeply ashamed. And really started to pray ...

But as I prayed, I was struck by the sheer selfishness and hypocrisy of how I was approaching God. I was ashamed of my academic performance. I recognised the need for help,,, any help at all. And I realised that I was praying in order to save face when I had a much deeper rooted problem,,, the problem of sin. That was the real issue I needed to address.

I do not recall now all the detail of the following months, but within the next couple of years I was able to say, 'Whereas I was blind, now I see'.

Prayer over the years has become a discipline and privilege that I have persevered and struggled with. I've written prayers, spoken out loud in prayer, prayed silently, prayed through Scripture, read others' prayers, used car journeys to pray. I've often based my prayers on the structure of The Lord's Prayer, I've used the idea of ACTS, Adoration, Confession, Thanksgiving, Supplications. I've sung the Psalms of David as prayers. These have all been strategies used to help this poor 'pray-er'.

In the final days of my late wife's life, I spent time by her bed praying quietly that the Lord would now gently take her home to her Eternal Rest. She had been ill for two and a half years. Morning and evening family worship continued as it had done throughout the prior thirty-seven years of marriage. The Scriptures we read, following the normal pattern we had established, were remarkably appropriate for our extreme time of need. A healing balm of Gilead to thirsty, needy souls.

The Psalms and hymns sung quietly and gently in these last days will forever live in my memory. She died after we had finished singing and praying:

Take my life, and let it be
Consecrated, Lord, to Thee;
Take my moments and my days,
Let them flow in ceaseless praise.
Let them flow in ceaseless praise.

Take my hands, and let them move
At the impulse of Thy love;
Take my feet, and let them be
Swift and beautiful for Thee.
Swift and beautiful for Thee.

Take my voice, and let me sing
Always, only, for my King;
Take my lips, and let them be
Filled with messages from Thee.
Filled with messages from Thee.

Take my silver and my gold:
Not a mite would I withhold;
Take my intellect, and use
Ev'ry pow'r as Thou shalt choose.
Ev'ry pow'r as Thou shalt choose.

Take my will, and make it Thine,
It shall be no longer mine;
Take my heart, it is Thine own,
It shall be Thy royal throne.
It shall be Thy royal throne.

Take my love, my Lord, I pour
At Thy feet its treasure store;
Take myself, and I will be,
Ever, only, all for Thee.
Ever, only, all for Thee.

   Frances Ridley Havergal, 1874

Lucille Travis

Lucille Travis is a freelance writer from Minnesota who has published fifteen children's books, most of them historical fiction. While her retired husband continues to teach seminary courses, Lucille keeps busy with her writing, and both are thankful for their church, their family, and most of all for the Lord whose love is steadfast.

I have always loved to read children's books like C. S. Lewis's Narnia tales and Tolkien's *Lord of the Rings* because they can so clearly portray Christian truth. Recently I read such a scene in Wayne Thomas Batson's *The Door Within*, that for me went right to the heart of prayer.

Briefly, a knight must pass his final test. Shall he choose the sword lying nearby or the scroll of the true King to face the powerful, and terrible thing at the door? He finally realizes, "I am no match for this thing even with a sword, I choose the scroll of the true King!" And he chose rightly.

I find myself, like that knight, saying, "my little strength, my small sword are not enough for this life; I need you, Lord." Prayer is all about choosing the true King who loves us and waits for us to come to him, to lay our needs before him, to trust his ways for us.

Another writer pictures our need for God like that of children at the end of the day longing for their father. What matters for me is that prayer is coming to our Heavenly Father, our God, our King, who loves us. It is far more than leaving a list of requests at his doorstep, though sadly, sometimes I have done that too. When I heard a radio pastor urge Christians to stop what he called "handing God the laundry list," and try praying through the Psalms, I wondered if it was really possible. I began praying through them each day one by one, and found far more than a method. What I found was a voice that brought me to the Lord to see what I often had not stopped to see, and to find exactly what I needed in my life.

Through the eyes of David, writer of so many of the Psalms, I saw God the Father—a picture of God so great, whose nature is so good and so loving he is willing to teach us, lead us, shelter us, bless us. How good it was to know that I could ask him to do those very things for me!

I saw myself –my own needs in David's cries to God. I saw the often helpless, sometimes wretchedness of my own humanity. And always there at the same time was the help the Lord offers, forgiveness and cleansing, and the sure knowledge that he will restore. What God pointed out and what he promised led to prayer for those things.

Prayer includes love, thankfulness, worship, and in the Psalms I saw this world, God's creation, upheld by him, a time for marveling. I saw the way to walk even in this fallen world, still his creation, under his sovereign hand. God sees the injustice in this world, the wickedness that I so well recognize, and his plans for both the wicked and the righteous quiet my heart.

Praying through the Psalms, like all prayer brings listening times, sometimes interrupting times when a promise of God from the Bible comes to mind, and always the time spent with the Lord, before him, is truly prayer. And you know it's far more than a method, this walk through the Psalms, more like a path you will never tire of taking. Not long ago I came home from a hospital stay, and found that about all I wanted to do was rest, no books, no cd's, just a nice collapse in my own welcome bed. And then I thought of praying through Psalm 23, the Shepherd Psalm familiar to most Christians. Slowly but surely I found the quiet waters waiting, and the Shepherd who restores souls, the feast even in the valley of the Shadow of Death, and the goodness and mercy did follow.

For me, the New Testament too is full of prayers meant for us to hear, examples for us to use. One is the Lord's Prayer that he taught his disciples to pray. It is a simple prayer that brings us before the Father, teaches us to ask his help each day, and reminds us to forgive others as we are forgiven. I find it is a great way to start each day.

Sometimes my prayers may be like David's, and sometimes there may be only a heart's desperate cry to the Lord, like the thief on the cross, "Remember me, O Lord." What matters most to me is to choose the true King who loves us and says, "Come."

Prayer Quotes

'Satan trembles when he sees the weakest Christian on his knees.' *William Cowper*

'You may as soon find a living man that does not breath, as a living Christian that does not pray.' *Matthew Henry*

'Prayer will make a man cease from sin, or sin will entice a man to cease from prayer.' *John Bunyan*

'Prayer is not overcoming God's reluctance, but laying hold of His willingness.' *Martin Luther*

'Prayer should not be regarded "as a duty which must be performed, but rather as a privilege to be enjoyed, a rare delight that is always revealing some new beauty."' *E.M. Bounds*

'Our prayer must not be self-centered. It must arise not only because we feel our own need as a burden we must lay upon God, but also because we are so bound up in love for our fellow men that we feel their need as acutely as our own. To make intercession for men is the most powerful and practical way in which we can express our love for them.' *John Calvin*

Magdolna McAlister

Magdolna McAlister is a Social Worker. She trained in her home country Romania, and has worked in this field for the last eleven years. She now lives in East Ayrshire, Scotland and enjoys being a full time wife and mother. Magdolna and her five year old daughter are waiting, God willing, for her husband's kidney transplant. She has entitled her article: God is God and God is Good.

God is God and God is good. These are not my words, but my husband's. Duncan came across them, through a video from the internet last year a few days before he was hospitalised with a serious kidney infection.

Duncan had Adult Polycystic Kidney Disease and after contracting a kidney infection and being infected by E-coli, his state had deteriorated so much that one of his kidneys had to be removed on 2nd March 2011.

I remember how angry I was at that time as I felt it was so unjust to see Duncan seriously ill. Our almost four-year-old adopted daughter needed her Daddy. Everything seemed to be so bleak and hopeless.

At that time we lived in Romania, and we had already known for a few months that things were not right with Duncan's health, and we were gearing up for a kidney transplant in Scotland later that year. However, God had a very different plan for us and allowed us to experience His love and faithfulness in a very special way.

During those sleepless nights in hospital, I would take Duncan for long walks in a wheelchair. He could not sleep because of the pain caused by his infected kidneys and I remember often crying out to the Lord and pleading with Him for my husband's life.

Duncan was always peaceful and while I was encouraging him to fight for his life he told me, '*Whatever God wants for me will be the best, and if I need to go, I go with peace in my heart. God knows better.*' Duncan just kept saying over and over, '*God is God and God is good.*' Slowly it became our life's principle – one that I struggled to accept – but deep in my heart I knew it was right.

Just a night before his operation a song came to my mind, and I could not think of anything else but this song, by Don Moen:

God will make a way, where there seems to be no way,
He works in ways we cannot see,
He will make a way for me.

Next day the operation was scheduled for 10 a.m. but Duncan was only taken to the operation theatre at about 1 p.m. During this time we had the opportunity to stay together in the ward by ourselves, praying and talking and waiting with my best friend. I should mention that a night before I had to phone our daughter and explain to her that Daddy was very ill and needed a big operation. She asked, '*But Mummy what happens if Daddy doesn't get better?*' Here, I had to be strong and tell her the truth, '*If Daddy doesn't get better, he will die and go to be with the Lord Jesus.*' This was a real breakthrough, as it helped me to accept the fact which Duncan had accepted well before me, that though we pray for healing and recovery, we have to accept that God might have a different plan for our lives.

Just a few hours before the surgery, Duncan gave his wedding ring back to me and we both prayed and thanked God for each other and for all the blessings we had had until then. We were ready to accept whatever God wanted to offer us, knowing that *God is God and He is good*, no matter what happened next. We also read Psalm 23, and then he was taken away about 1 p.m. I remained behind, knowing that from New Zealand to Africa and from the U.S.A. to many other European countries, not to mention the U.K. and Romania, family, friends and brothers and sisters in Christ were all praying for us. This knowledge gave me peace and a kind of joy that I cannot explain under the circumstances, but I can only thank my Heavenly Father for it.

About 2.30 p.m. I was called up to the operating theatre where I was informed that they needed my signature, as Duncan had only a 30 % chance of survival and his own agreement was not enough for the operation. This was the last opportunity for me to see Duncan before the surgery. There was just enough time to send him a kiss and tell him how much we loved him.

God listened to our prayers according to our hearts' desire and Duncan had his first successful operation and his left kidney was removed. After the operation, whilst Duncan was in intensive care, four people died next to him within eight days. This was very distressing for him. However, we believed he was in the right place at the right time, as he kept praying for each person during their struggle while they passed away. At that point I realized that Duncan was on a mission field even in intensive care.

Since then, Duncan's right kidney has been removed too, and now we live in Scotland, waiting for a kidney transplant. Duncan's brother will be the donor, God willing. During the past sixteen months we have both experienced God's amazing love and I am convinced that whatever has happened in our lives was proof that even today God listens to His people's cries.

People keep asking me how I am coping and sometimes they pity me. However, I have to confess that though this was one of the toughest periods in my life, I do feel privileged and I know that I have a great God who has amazing ways to show His love towards His children. Through the suffering and difficult times I have been able to see His loving care and feel sheltered, knowing that His faithfulness is greater than my unbelief and doubts. Whatever happens in our lives, happens according to His plan, which is the best for us.

We don't know what the future holds for us, but we know a few things: miracles do happen even today, the Holy Spirit works as a great Comforter, and we are very blessed that through Jesus Christ we can call God, 'Abba Father'!

Our lives have certainly received a new meaning and God has an amazing way of teaching us how to appreciate each other and everything else that is offered to us. We know everything is given only for a time and we ought to be faithful stewards and remind ourselves that each moment of life is a gift and it is our responsibility how we use this gift.

One of the greatest lessons I have learned through this journey is that God is God above all circumstances, and He never plays with our feelings. Things might go from bad to worse but we have a God whose faithfulness is eternal and whose love is unchangeable. Our families' and friends' prayers deeply touched us and I know that because these prayers were listened to, I had the strength to go on. In fact, it was just like the situation with Aaron, Hur and Moses – when I got tired and weary, my hands were held up by my brothers and sisters in Christ.

Maureen Ross

Maureen Ross has worked in tele-sales for Christian Focus Publications and is actively involved in her local community of the Seaboard; three small fishing villages on the east coast of Scotland. She enjoys listening and participating in music... something that she has passed on through the generations to her children and grandchildren.

I get great pleasure in reminiscing so this is a good opportunity to look back on my earliest memories of prayer in my life. It has been quite an encouragement to realise just how the Lord's hand had been moving long before I was aware of my need of Him.

One of my earliest memories was when I was about five years old, (and it remains to this day a treasured memory from my childhood). I had two plaques, consisting of a picture and a prayer. I can still clearly visualize them standing on my kidney shaped dressing table, one on either side.

The plaque on the left was a picture of a little curly blond haired girl in her nightgown ready to go to bed, kneeling down and resting her elbows on the bed with her hands clasped in prayer. The prayer written below was:-

As I lay down my head to sleep
I pray the Lord my soul to keep.
If I should die before I wake
I pray the Lord my soul to take.

On the right was a picture of a Shepherd walking down from the hills, with a strong bright light around him. You got the sense he was almost about to walk out of the picture. He held a shepherd's crook in one hand and around his neck, almost like a scarf, was a little lamb held by the feet. That prayer said:-

Gentle Jesus meek and mild,
Look upon this little child,
Pity my simplicity,
And suffer me to come to thee.

These prayers were easy to memorise, and as a child I prayed these prayers over and over again. Did those plaques provoke interest and raise questions over the years? I believe they did because I would often think of them, pray them out loud and to myself. I know that I grew up believing that God existed and instinctively prayed to Him believing He was hearing my prayers.

My parents were not Christians. Although Mam would occasionally take us to church, we certainly did not have family worship or such at home, There is no explanation as to why as a child I had a leaning towards God other than His hand was upon me.

Another strong and impacting memory was from my school days. There would always be Morning Assembly, when the school day began with the singing of a Psalm, paraphrase or hymn, followed by a reading, and finally the Lord's Prayer.

The Lord's Prayer was said in parrot fashion, but even learning this way I found was of great benefit. Looking back I am grateful for all those Morning Assemblies, often these are the portions of Scripture which come so readily to mind.

But how did I move on from the childish verses and the parrot like prayer recitals? Well, an old friend of my parents, Maggie Jane, (we as children called her Aunty Meg, although she was not really an aunt) often stayed with us. She was quite a character and when she came to visit she shared my room. Aunty Meg went through the same ritual every night. Firstly, she would plaster her face with Nivea face cream, and I mean plaster! Then she would put a few curlers in her hair, get into bed, make herself comfortable and ask me to read a few verses from the Bible followed by prayer. Meg would tell me of things to pray about and I would also add my own petitions. This helped me to move on from my two plaque prayers and repeating the Lord's Prayer parrot fashion.

Aunty Meg would then say it was time for me to go to sleep whilst she sat up with the light full on reading the daily newspaper – it's not easy getting to sleep listening to the racket of rustling newspapers right next to you!

These memories from my childhood give a glimpse into how prayer can impact us from a very early age. Could I go a day without prayer? I don't think so, and I certainly don't want to try. Prayer is essential. If as a Christian you are not praying then you must question and examine yourself, as prayer is the Christian's way of expressing and acknowledging dependence on God. It says in the Bible that God delights in our prayers. We can speak to Him and 'tell all', thanking Him for what He has done. We can pray anytime and anywhere. I am not saying we will always like the answer, but we can be sure the answer is the right one for us.

I do not know who bought me these two plaques, but I am eternally grateful for them. It is amazing what the Lord uses to bring us to Himself.

Holy Breathings

The true spirit of prayer is no other than God's own Spirit dwelling in the hearts of the saints. And as this spirit comes from God, so doth it naturally tend to God in holy breathings and pantings. It naturally leads to God, to converse with him by prayer.

Jonathan Edwards

Nancy Messner

Nancy Messner is a home-schooling mother of five and is married to a Chaplain/Pastor (Rev. Aaron Messner.) She earned a BA and MA from Wheaton College, Wheaton, IL, the latter in Clinical Psychology. She and her husband currently live in Georgia. She has entitled her article: The Impact of Prayer to the One True God.

Many in the world today view prayer as a practice that does neither tremendous good, nor any real harm. General opinion in much of the western world is that prayer is acceptable and an expression of good will and promotes mutual respect between community members. Prayer is commonly in place at weddings, inaugurations, graduations, and the like without too much criticism from the general public. It is something allowable as a part of ceremony in many cultures around the world. It is an accepted tradition. Perhaps even members of society who do not consider themselves to be "religious" do find prayer in these settings acceptable and allowable. It is a nicety.

While this casual acceptance of prayer is on the surface, benign, it is precisely the reason why many view prayer as a pithy substitute for action and ascribe it little value. Prayer is seen as decent, moral, but not effectual. Prayer is lovely and decorative, but not influential. It is allowed but not cherished nor depended upon.

This devaluing of prayer is a direct and logical result of a grave misunderstanding of prayer itself. Prayer is neither safe, nor quaint. Neither can prayer be manipulated by any mere human—used at a whim for his or her own purposes. Prayer is purposeful, striking, and an evidence of real power.

Prayer is a tool but it is also a weapon that wields great power. It is indeed dangerous for those who attempt its use in ignorance. Fire is a tool, but can cause death in the hands of one who is ignorant of its nature and qualities.

So, how can we come to have a proper understanding and use of this wondrous weapon called prayer? Can this proper understanding of prayer equip us to wield real power and produce meaningful results in our lives?

Prayer accomplishes so much more than mere oration or even communication as we know it to be between human beings. Although prayer does include our thoughts directed toward someone, human communication pales in comparison with the mystical communion experienced when we make contact with the one, true God.

There are important reasons why this is so. The true God whom we speak of here is a being of a specific, fixed character. He is never failing, never alters, and never unavailable. We are conversing with a solid rock who is not of our own creation. We do not speak in our own imaginations when we pray, appealing to a nebulous morphing cloud. We direct this communication to a supernatural being, one with objective qualities, actual responses. God has opinions.

Not only does God have opinions, but he has had them since even before the creation of the world. He is and has been active in this world in all of history. All wisdom, knowledge, and power dwells within this being, God. It is unfathomable that we can take prayer so lightly!

God is holy, and as he is set apart and separate from his people, his people must take special care and diligence in giving him the honor and reverence he is due. As he has opinions and a fixed character, he has opinions of how we pray. He has shown us in his Scriptures how to address him. If we, his people, do not heed these guidelines we expose our overall opinion of God himself. This is precisely why prayer can be dangerous. How we pray exposes our view of God and we risk offending him with the haughtiness we exhibit.

The mere acknowledgement of God's character may cause us to doubt that communication, this mystical communion is even possible with people like us. And, in fact, it is not possible for everyone.

The God of the universe does not bestow the power of prayer lightly, nor easily. The privilege of conversing and communing with a holy God is reserved for his chosen people for the purpose of his eternal glory. These chosen people are the ones who have claimed Jesus Christ as Lord, and claimed redemption by his atoning sacrifice on the cross. Only those who have been redeemed by Christ can approach his throne through prayer. He must clean us and make us his own before we can speak with him. And, only his people can speak his language. Only his own children can recognize the voice of their father.

As a father loves his children and wants to dwell with and know them, God also desires to love, dwell, and know his people. Prayer is the way that this is accomplished. As this occurs, God is glorified.

He is glorified as we petition him for help and as we agonize in prayer for our neighbors. He is glorified as we thank him and as we seek him with our questions. His Word says that he hears our prayers and answers them as a kind father, a giver of good gifts.

Would a Father-God be satisfied with polite wishes and superstitious incantations? Would a God who sacrificed his own son for the redemption, purchase, and adoption of these children be satisfied with mere nicety and banter?

God is certainly not content with prayer as a traditional embellishment. He has designed it to be so much more. Not only does a process of "request and answer" occur through prayer, a transformation actually takes place. More than just two-way communication, prayer makes the most change in the one who prays. As the believer communes with his Father-God he does not merely express his own will, but as his prayers are directed by the words of Scripture, his will is transformed into a likeness of God's own will. The wishes, desires, hopes and dreams of the believer become aligned with God's. In essence, prayer transforms the heart and soul of the one who sincerely and faithfully prays.

Herein lies the true power of prayer. It is a dynamic, relational, supernatural communication in which the creator deigns to converse with his creatures, be moved by their complaints, and yet continually conforms them to his own purposes. He grants to us the privilege of wielding this powerful weapon of prayer as a part of his perfect ultimate design and purpose of kingdom building. With the final kingdom as the ultimate goal, there is no prayer that, when aligned with God's will, will ever be ineffectual or impotent. We will be witnesses to amazing changes. We will not fail to observe the unmistakable imprint of God's own actions upon our lives and our world. If you have not already witnessed this undeniable working power, open your eyes, and prepare to be amazed at what God does through prayer.

Nicole Watson

Nicole Watson resides in Longreach, outback Australia. She is a wife, mother, author, public speaker and teacher. It is her great honour to serve God and family using these gifts.

Prayer is more important to me than the very air I breathe. I sometimes sit back and wonder at how I ever stumbled through life without being in love with my God. So tangible and essential is our relationship, that the everyday becomes the extraordinary, all through prayer spoken and answered by a faithful God.

In recent years my life was radically transformed and refined by fire. Our youngest son Sam was born with a rare form of congenital heart disease; in essence he lives with half a heart. In crisis, one of two paths are chosen. People either choose to run from God, or run with fervour into his arms. I chose the latter, trusting him for all things at all times. I have seen his miraculous hand at work in our lives and in the lives of others. His mercy and power are unending and his love knows no bounds. God's Kingdom and his power walk hand in hand with our prayer and trust in him.

One such example of God's answer to prayer in our own lives occurred when my son Sam was only one year old. One morning Sam awoke not being able to move his arm. It hung limply by his side and when I tried to lift it, it simply fell back down. As panic began to rise in my chest, I asked the Lord, *'What is this? What do I do?'* I felt strongly led to take Sam to the hospital, so packing him into the car along with my three year old son, we drove the twenty minutes to the hospital with haste. As I drove I prayed aloud and with passion stirred by a mother's love. *"Touch his arm Father, restore the movement Lord! Heal him by the blood of Jesus and power of my testimony. You have given me a promise for his life Lord and I remind you of it now. Sam will hold and drink his bottle with both hands. He will play with his toys with both hands. He will clap and dance and sing with both hands. He will raise both hands in worship to you. I claim all of this in Jesus' name!"* Every time I would say the name of Jesus, my eldest son would shout it too.

By the time we arrived at the hospital emergency department Sam's arm had started to twitch rhythmically. We were admitted quickly due to Sam's cardiac condition and proceeded to wait for three hours in the emergency department. Doctors came and went. When the fourth doctor entered to examine him, Sam lifted his arm and placed it onto my shoulder. I jumped and shouted with excitement! God had healed his arm. Much later that night, after tests and an MRI, the doctors found that Sam had indeed suffered a stroke, and that he should not be moving his arm. Sam left the hospital five days later with no effects from his stroke whatsoever. The doctors kept expecting him to regress, but God's healing power was complete. Teams of specialists would come and visit us at Sam's bedside and ask me to tell them the story again. The doctors would look at his chart and then they would just stare at him in amazement and confusion. They told us he would perhaps have problems with his speech and development. Never once has he looked back from the incident. Sam was completely cleared by the doctors and has never had to go back to see them again. He is now four years old and speaks with great confidence.

Sam still lives with only half a heart but God has given us a promise for his life. Sam will live and have life in abundance. *He will testify of his healing to the nations.* And God's promises are true and steadfast. We must live the life and plan that God has prepared for us since before time began. Prayer is more than mere words. Prayer is the key to a living, loving and life transforming relationship with our Creator. I pray while I wash the dishes, sing to him in the shower, and in the car. I pray with our children, with my husband and for them as well. Prayer allows God to work in our lives the way he has always wanted to. Prayer is our invitation to our Father, inviting him to take the lead and pour out his power into our lives. The world would have us render prayer as useless, words thrown into the air, with little purpose. God's Word tells us differently, and on that truth we must stand without doubt. I have seen the mountain thrown into the sea, and nothing in this world can make me doubt my God and his promises. Trust him with your life, trust him with your heart's most hidden desires, trust him with your most precious treasures and be prepared to be undone by the absolute love that he has for you. God will use your smallest prayer to bring glory to his name and change lives forever.

A Desire for God Himself

"The essence of prayer does not consist in asking God for something but in opening our hearts to God, in speaking with Him, and living with Him in perpetual communion. Prayer is continual abandonment to God. Prayer does not mean asking God for all kinds of things we want; it is rather the desire for God Himself, the only Giver of Life. Prayer is not asking, but union with God. Prayer is not a painful effort to gain from God help in the varying needs of our lives. Prayer is the desire to possess God Himself, the Source of all life. The true spirit of prayer does not consist in asking for blessings, but in receiving Him who is the giver of all blessings, and in living a life of fellowship with Him."

Sadhu Sundar Singh

Patrick Sookhdeo

Dr Patrick Sookhdeo was born in Guyana, South America, and now lives in the U.K. He studied theology at the then London Bible College, where he met his wife, Rosemary, from New Zealand. For many years he was an evangelist, church-planter and pastor, and is now International Director of Barnabas Fund, an aid agency to assist persecuted Christians.

As a young boy growing up in a Muslim home and attending the mosque, I was taught to pray. For prayer is one of the Five Pillars of Islam and therefore an obligatory duty. Yet, it was prayer to a god whom I did not know, a god who was distant and far away. I could never be sure that he was hearing my prayers, or that he would answer them.

Yet, there were occasions where somehow God did intervene. Once when my father was taken off to prison, my mother had nothing for the family to eat. I was walking along the road on a very, very hot day, with no water on either side, praying to God for food for my mother, when at my feet suddenly I saw a fish, alive, which I took home and we ate.

When I came to the U.K. and first heard the gospel as a young student, I began to attend church every Sunday. And I began to pray a different prayer. I knew that God existed but wanted desperately to know whether He could be known, and so I would pray every day, 'God, if you are there, reveal yourself to me.' At the end of six months of praying this, I not only came to the realisation that God is, that He exists, but also

I came to know Him in the person of His Son Jesus Christ whom He revealed to me. God was no longer a distant deity, a far removed entity, but was now someone who resided within me, who even made His home in my heart. He was one whom I now knew personally and intimately, whom I could walk with, who would carry all my burdens.

It was not easy to be a Christian from a Muslim background. Living as a tramp during one period, without home or food, praying became part of life. But the knowledge of God's presence carried me through those very difficult days. And when the temptation to end it all proved almost too much, God always intervened.

I have now been in Christian ministry for 43 years, and the knowledge that God is the source not only of my belief but also of all aid and comfort, support and help, guidance, counselling and instruction has never been more important. My wife and I lived as faith missionaries for many years. We had to learn to trust God for our day to day support and existence. We brought up our children without a regular salary to provide for them, depending only on God through His people for our daily needs. We had many experiences of divine intervention, of how God came and provided at the exact moment of need.

Furthermore, being in ministry and carrying a work of God (including the support of my ministry colleagues) and in latter years an aid agency, constantly makes me realise anew how important it is to pray. For in situations of economic decline, when all around things may well be collapsing and when predictions for the future are universally grim, the temptation to despair always exists. Yet prayer becomes the antidote to despair. It is prayer that fuels hope and confidence because it takes us into the Father's presence, with the knowledge that our Father knows best and that He will provide and He will support.

Over the years, I have had to travel extensively for the ministry, sometimes in situations of conflict and potential danger. Here again prayer becomes operative. Once when I was visiting Pakistan, I arrived at Karachi airport in the early hours and took a taxi to the place where I was to stay. But the taxi driver seemed to have mischief in mind. As I prayed for deliverance, the taxi came to a halt in a long line of traffic where all the vehicles turned off their lights (a Pakistani custom that I can never understand). A motorcyclist drew alongside my taxi in pitch darkness and said to me in perfect English, "Where do you want to go?" I blurted out that I did not trust the taxi driver, and I explained whom I was trying to visit. The motorcyclist replied, "I know him." He then told the taxi driver in Urdu to follow him. The taxi driver kept trying to lose the motorcycle, but each time the rider would double back and pick up the taxi again. When we arrived at the place, I turned to thank him and he had disappeared. God in His mercy had intervened. He had heard my prayers and brought deliverance.

Prayer has become not just a formalised routine but increasingly the very basis of my existence, whether in waking or sleeping, in walking or in discussion. The mind must constantly be brought back to Him, often with small, silent prayers, knowing that God is not only present but involved. Liturgical prayer is valuable for it embeds within the heart and the mind prayers that can be used when all else fails or when the mind is too weary to concentrate, for example, during long distance travel. Here the Lord's Prayer becomes invaluable. Also, using a structured format such as ACTS – adoration, confession, thanksgiving, supplication – helps as it can formulate a pattern, particularly useful when it is difficult to pray. In moments of tiredness I often look at my hand, and use that as guidance for prayer. The thumb speaks of God, for without the thumb, what can the hand do, and without God what can we do? The index finger, the nearest to me, reminds me to pray for those nearest and dearest in my life. The middle finger, the strongest, is a prompter to pray for those in authority in the Church and government. The ring finger, the weakest, speaks of praying for the sick and suffering, not forgetting vulnerable and persecuted Christians. Finally, I reach the little finger, the smallest, which is when I pray for myself.

But for most of life it is the extempore prayer, the talking to the Lord, the moments with Him in the quietness that give life and sustenance.

Penny Reeve

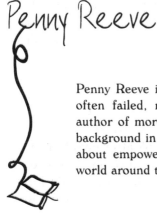

Penny Reeve is a wife, mother of three and stubborn, often failed, resister of the busy-culture. She is the author of more than eleven children's books and has a background in teaching and missions. She is passionate about empowering children to respond in faith to the world around them, and rest in the deep love of God.

I am a child. Tired and sore.

I've tripped and hurt my knee. Red stuff seeps from gravel stripes and my eyes are going blurry.

'*Come here, little one,*' I hear the voice of one who loves me.

But I'm too busy. I shove aside the other children and grab as many stale crackers as I can, making sure, by my own strength, that I will get enough.

And then I slip, the crackers fall and my blurry eyes begin to cry. I cannot see the beetles now. I can't even hear the magpies. I'm hungry, thirsty, wretched and lonely out here among all my friends.

'*Come here,*' the voice calls again. And this time I stop.

I lift my face.

The one that calls me is my Father. I know that he has soothing cream, and bandages to keep my 'ouchy' safe. There's a cuddle and a kiss and something good to eat. He'll wipe my smeary face. He'll hold my pain and draw me close. But can I go? Will I try?

***

Prayer, to me – a child of God – is a lot more than heads down, eyes closed, words thrown into the waiting space. Prayer is like a breath – sucked in desperation as I lunge up out of the murk of everyday life. I am like the little child described above; so busy doing this and that and the other. I make lunches, drive the school run, try to out-wit the toddler, squeeze in creative thought, remember to cook dinner, attempt to live simply only to find my life cluttered and in havoc. I find myself drained and weary with a collection of little 'ouchies' I haven't bothered taking to my Father to tend. I can see, when I pause long enough, that my human instinct is to look after myself. I've got to fight. I've got to protect my interests. I've got to prove my point. But in doing so, I'm effectively holding my breath. Life is gradually suffocated, hope dries up and all power – every little ounce of it my own – is used up, spent, worn out and perishing.

But prayer. Oh, prayer! It's where the end of me meets the completeness of Christ. Prayer is like a teeny, tiny, baby step compared to the mighty gulf-spanning work of the cross. For reconciliation comes from God alone. It is through faith that we are saved – not by anything we could do or say or make or write – and prayer is just a tiny nudge on our behalf. '*Draw near to God*', James urges us, '*and God will draw near to you*' (James 4:7). So the little child in me lifts her head and draws a breath. Sometimes that's all I can manage. It's a bare shift of stance, an admission that I need more than me; but even in that tiny act God draws near to listen.

My words can be a traditional formulation, or a messy gush of emotion. God can handle what I say, and I rest in the knowledge that when my words are less than adequate, my Heavenly Father knows my heart completely. He doesn't demand or expect the 'right words' for every situation. I wonder sometimes if he even wants them. The child in me draws even closer now and I find myself in his shadow.

Oh, what a mighty shadow it is! Standing here, carrying my little bundles of concern, I realise just how small they are compared to his mighty hands. But God doesn't scoff at me. He doesn't mock my snuffly tears. No, he holds them. He knows each one and each one's cause. In prayer I bring my burdens into that wonderful shade and begin to unpack them. Bit by bit, as I'm ready, as he gently suggests. And each time I do so, I understand a fragment more of what my salvation means.

Because prayer also reminds me of my inadequacies. I suddenly see the gap between who I am and who Christ is, and it's so desperately wide. If I lower my gaze from my Father's face now I'll only hear my own voice, or the voices of others around me, telling me that I am something of a failure. But God doesn't use those words when talking about me. He cups my chin, turns my face upwards and, using the fabric of pure righteousness, wipes my tears away. Then he tells me truth, *always* the truth: that I was bought at a great price. For *his* glory.

And I am speechless. The clamouring noises of my life are gently muted. Devotion wells from a deep place I didn't even know I had. The scabby knee seems strangely worth it – if only to get to this position.

But the world continues to bustle and crave and heave and sob around me and so my Loving Almighty Father gently turns me around again. He dusts me off, reminds me my bundles are in good hands and squeezes my hand before sending me out again.

So I go. But in prayer I keep looking back, over my shoulder, to see him watching me, suggesting obstacles to overcome and caring for all I've given him. Yes, I've still got my 'ouchies', but he's got them covered. I still feel tired, but he gives me strength. I know I'll trip up again. Probably very soon too. But God will be there to hold my hand and lift me from the dirt.

***

'Come,' I hear my Father call.

So I turn to the nearest, grubby faced child beside me and ask the obvious question: *'You wanna come too?'*

Rebecca VanDoodewaard

Rebecca VanDoodewaard was born into a family of ministers. By God's grace, this did not inoculate her against the gospel but has strengthened her in it. Seeking to pass on the faith to her children, she is thankful that regeneration is up to the Spirit, not her. Amazingly, her favourite professor, writer, and preacher is also her husband.

P rayer has impacted my life more than I know. God has used prayer so pivotally to change me that I can only see part of it right now. But even the part that I can see is substantial.

He has used the prayers of my grandparents in my life. All four of them lifted me up before the Throne before I was born, pleading for my safe arrival in this world and a faithful pilgrimage to the next. Three of them still remember me daily in prayer, as they watch a granddaughter walk through stages of life that they mastered decades ago. This is so humbling. A praying grandparent is a powerful person.

God has used the prayers of my parents in my life. They also started praying for me before I was born, but prayed with greater fervency once I arrived – I was a difficult child! God answered their prayers and saved me from His wrath against my sin for the sake of Christ's atonement. God was faithful to hear the pleas of believing parents. And they not only prayed for me, but also with me, teaching me to come often before God in prayer, bringing thanks and needs to Him as they arose.

These patterns of prayer have continued as I grew up and left their home. The influence of my parents' early instruction will continue for life.

God has used the prayers of my husband in my life. Before I knew he was interested in me, he was praying for me. On our second date, he began praying with and for me. To hear him praise God for me and intercede for me day after day, and to be able to do the same for him, has given our marriage a stability and security that it would not otherwise have. I know that he loves my soul in a deep way, expressed in his prayers for me. Praying for a spouse is one of the biggest ways to care for their soul.

God has used the prayers of the saints in my life. From aunts and uncles to acquaintances, the prayers of God's people for me have worked deeply, usually without my realizing what is happening spiritually until it is over and I look back. When I was a child, many of the adults in my congregation prayed for my salvation – partly in compassion for my distressed parents! Later, they prayed for my spiritual health as I finished high school and attended a secular university. Since then, prayers for safe travels, births, wisdom to parent, faithfulness to minister, and more, have gone up to the Throne on my behalf. Knowing that so many people have given their thought and time to my spiritual health is something that puts me in my proper, tiny place. I am part of a body, and a universal one at that. I need it more than I realize. The saints themselves probably do not realize how much of an impact their prayers have had.

God has used prayer itself to shape my life. As I learn and relearn the basics of this other-worldly practice, the Lord teaches me to wait on Him, to accept His answers as wiser than my requests, and to ask for what He has promised in His Word to give. My own sin draws me near to the throne of grace to receive mercy and find grace in time of need (Heb. 4:16). God's goodness and love prompt me to bring sacrifices of praise (Jer. 33:11). Waiting to see how and when God answers requests has taught me invaluable spiritual lessons: God is good beyond my comprehension, and so patient with my unbelief.

Most of all, God the Father has used the prayers of the Son in my life. Without my Saviour's intercessions, all the other prayers would be useless. And the prayers of Christ go far beyond the prayers of any mortal not only in their acceptability before God, but also in their depth and breadth. Without the prayers of any other people, Jesus' prayers would be sufficient for me, as He intercedes with God on my behalf. Who can comprehend or explain the impact of Messiah's prayers on our behalf?

> When I stand before the throne,
> Dressed in beauty not my own,
> When I see Thee as Thou art,
> Love Thee with unsinning heart,
> Then, Lord, shall I fully know,
> Not 'till then, how much I owe.
> *Robert Murray McCheyne, 1837*

Prayer Quotes

'As it is the business of tailors to make clothes and cobblers to make shoes, so it is the business of Christians to pray.' *Martin Luther*

'Each time, before you intercede, be quiet first, and worship God in His glory. Think of what He can do, and how He delights to hear the prayers of His redeemed people. Think of your place and privilege in Christ, and expect great things!' *Andrew Murray*

'Prayer is where the action is.' *John Wesley*

'Don't pray when you feel like it. Have an appointment with the Lord and keep it. A man is powerful on his knees.' *Corrie ten Boom*

'Trouble and perplexity drive me to prayer and prayer drives away perplexity and trouble.' *Philip Melanchthon*

'Prayer does not mean simply to pour out one's heart. It means rather to find the way to God and to speak with him, whether the heart is full or empty.' *Dietrich Bonhoeffer*

Robin Sydserff

Robin Sydserff is minister of St. Catherine's Church of Scotland in Edinburgh. He is married to Sally and they have three children.

While the Bible is full of inspirational and practical teaching on prayer, a passage I've found particularly helpful, both personally and in encouraging others, is Luke 10:38–11:13, the familiar story of Martha and Mary (10:38-42), followed by Jesus' teaching on prayer (11:1-13). In this section of his Gospel, Luke, the writer, has been explaining that followers of Jesus are to be marked by love – love for the Lord and love for our neighbour. It's that first dimension, love for the Lord, that Luke is concerned with in 10:38-11:13. We are to love the Lord by listening to him and speaking to him.

Loving the Lord by listening to him (Luke 10:38-42 NIV)

The key to loving the Lord is listening to him rather than doing things for him. Picture the scene! Jesus comes to town and Martha opens her home to him. She takes her responsibilities as hostess extremely seriously and busies herself with all the preparations. She wants to do her very best for Jesus, her motivation genuine and sincere. Her sister Mary, though, had other ideas. Mary 'sat at the Lord's feet listening to what he said' (v. 39). Martha is busy about the house with all that needs done while Mary is sitting at Jesus' feet listening to his teaching. And Martha is not best pleased! She's annoyed with her sister, and also it seems with Jesus: 'She came to [Jesus] and asked, "Lord, don't you care that my sister has left me to do the work by myself? Tell her to help me!"' (v. 40) Strong words! Jesus' reply is kind and gentle, but absolutely clear: "Martha, Martha ... you are worried and upset about many things, but only one thing is needed. Mary has chosen what is better, and it will not be taken away from her" (vv. 41-42). Obviously, we can't sit at the feet of Jesus in the way Mary did, so how do we listen to Jesus? We listen to Jesus through the Bible. We encounter the living Word through the written Word. When does this happen? Sunday by Sunday as the Bible is read and preached and when we study the Bible with others in small groups. But just as important is the daily rhythm of reading our Bibles, spending time alone with God in his Word.

Loving the Lord by speaking to him (Luke 11:1-13 NIV)

Loving the Lord means listening to him and also speaking to him. In response to a question from the disciples (v. 1) about how they should pray, Jesus offers some practical and helpful instruction.

(i) A pattern for our praying (Luke 11:2-4 NIV)

First, he suggests a pattern to shape the content of our prayers:

> When you pray, say:
> 'Father,
> hallowed be your name,
> your kingdom come.
> Give us each day our daily bread.
> Forgive us our sins,
> for we also forgive everyone who sins
> against us.
> And lead us not into temptation' (Luke 11:2-4).

Often referred to as 'The Lord's Prayer' (Matthew has a slightly longer version (Matt. 6:9-13)), as a title this is perhaps misleading. Jesus' intention is not primarily to give us a set prayer (although it's certainly appropriate to pray these words), so much as to teach us a pattern for prayer, a template, if you like, that we should use as a basis, expanding and amplifying as appropriate.

To pray 'hallowed be your name' is to pray for the reputation, the honour of God. To pray 'your kingdom come' is to pray for the outworking of God's salvation plan in the world. It means to pray for the extension of God's Kingdom, the growth of the Church – people coming to faith, people growing in their faith, the purity of the Church. And it means to pray for the coming of God's everlasting Kingdom, the return of the Lord Jesus in glory.

And then the pattern for praying moves to our daily needs: daily provision – 'Give us each day our daily bread'; daily forgiveness and a spirit of forgiveness towards others – 'Forgive us our sins, for we also forgive everyone who sins against us'; and daily protection – 'And lead us not into temptation.'

This pattern helps us keep the right priorities in focus – God's reputation, his honour and evangelism our first concerns, and then our daily needs.

Maybe for some of us this regular habit of talking to God, praying to God each day has slipped. Maybe we've never had that rhythm in our lives. Maybe you're a new Christian and you're wondering what you should be praying to God each day. Here's a practical suggestion. Get a notebook and put as a heading at the top of each page: 'hallowed be your name'; 'your kingdom come', 'Give us each day our daily bread' etc. For each day work through the list, taking the principle as the basis for your prayers, amplifying / expanding in different ways. So, for example:

'hallowed be your name'
Day 1: Praying that the way I live my life would honour God.
Day 2: Praying that the church to which I belong would honour God.

'your kingdom come'
Day 1: Praying for boldness to tell the gospel to my friends, and for opportunities to do so.
Day 2: Praying for those in parts of the world facing persecution because of their faith.
'Give us each day our daily bread.'

Day 1: Thanking God for providing everything I need and acknowledging my dependence on him for everything.
Day 2: Asking for contentment with what I have, and a generous, willing heart to share what I don't need with others.
And so on ...

(ii) **Praying boldly, believing that God will answer our prayers with good things (Luke 11:5-13 NIV)**

Having taught us what to pray for, Jesus goes on to teach about our attitude in prayer (vv. 5-8). Using an illustration of a man knocking on his friend's door at midnight to get some bread to feed his guests, Jesus encourages us to pray boldly, petitioning God, motivated by and conscious of the very real responsibilities we have as Christians: '... yet because of the man's boldness he will get up and give him as much as he needs' (v. 8b). And so, for example, we are to pray with boldness for the reputation of God in the Church and for the salvation of our friends who are not Christians.

Having encouraged us to pray boldly, Jesus encourages us to pray believing that God will answer our prayers with good things. Verses 9 and 10 are wonderful verses: 'So I say to you: Ask and it will be given to you; seek and you will find; knock and the door will be opened to you. For everyone who asks receives; he who seeks finds; and to him who knocks, the door will be opened.' Jesus has in mind what he has just taught. Ask, seek in your prayers, in accordance with this pattern to shape your praying, and God will answer your prayers. Knock on the door, pray with boldness, and the door will be opened. What a wonderful promise, sufficient in itself to motivate us to pray. The closing verses in the section reiterate this point, almost as if Jesus doesn't think we believe him! 'If you then, though you are evil, know how to give good gifts to your children, how much more will your Father in heaven give the Holy Spirit to those who ask him!' (v. 13) Notice the focus on the giving of the Holy Spirit in answer to our prayers. What does Jesus mean? Simply, I think, daily grace to live by, daily grace in response to daily prayer.

Why is this so important?

Why is this so important? Think back to the wider context in

Luke's Gospel. If we're not listening and talking to him, then we're not loving the Lord. That's a sobering thought! And if we're not loving the Lord, if that first love grows cold, then all manner of things will begin to unwind in our Christian lives. All too soon we'll mirror Martha's critical spirit – critical of our fellow believers and critical of the Lord Jesus himself.

My friend and mentor, David Jackman, past President of The Proclamation Trust, said something at a conference that I've never forgotten: 'There's a danger that we become more devoted to the work of the Lord than to the Lord.' That's exactly what Luke is dealing with in this section of his Gospel – daily devotion to the Lord, sitting at his feet, listening to him and talking to him. Indispensable habits for the Christian life.

Lisping and Shouting

Prayer is the lisping of the believing infant, the shout of the fighting believer, the requiem of the dying saint falling asleep in Jesus. It is the breath, the watchword, the comfort, the strength, the honour of a Christian. If thou be a child of God, thou wilt seek thy Father's face, and live in thy Father's love. Pray that this year thou mayest be holy, humble, zealous, and patient; have closer communion with Christ, and enter oftener into the banqueting-house of His love.

Charles Spurgeon,
Morning and Evening

Roger Carswell

Roger is a Yorkshire-based, travelling evangelist. Married, with four children, his passion is that everyone should hear and understand the gospel of Jesus and His love.

Before my conversion prayer was something to be done in church, school, before meals and in an emergency situation. I remember praying whilst in the dentist's chair that what was about to happen would not hurt, and on entering an exam room that, even though I hadn't revised much, God would help me get good marks. Neither prayer seemed to work!

When on holiday in the Lebanon as a 15 year old, and staying with Christian relatives who worked there, one of them took time to explain to me the gospel. Sitting on a log in a clearing in the woods in the Lebanese mountains, he used the Book of Romans to outline the way of salvation. I had never before understood that Jesus had died bearing my sin in His own body. If He loved me enough to die for me then I should trust Him as my Lord and Saviour, and ask Him to bring me to know God. Praying a prayer and calling on Jesus to forgive me, and, by His Spirit, come to live in my life, brought me to know the true and living God. It was the hinge which changed the very direction of my life, and made all things new.

My uncle who led me to Christ, urged me to make an appointment with God each day, and spend time reading His Word as well as praying to Him. He urged me to never keep God waiting, but be in that place at that time each day. Regretfully, the irregularity of my life has meant that that has not happened. However, I have sought to cultivate and keep the daily, dogged, delightful discipline of a 'quiet time' with the Lord. As well as Bible reading and prayer, I will sometimes sing or read a hymn, so as to tune my heart in preparation for my time with Him. I am reminded that the evidence that Saul of Tarsus had been converted was that he prayed (see Acts 9:11). For me too, it was one of the earliest marks of my new life in Christ.

George Müller, testified at the end of his life to having had 25,000 specific answers to prayer. I cannot make such a claim, but I have known God answer numerous specific prayers, and sometimes in ways that I could never have imagined or devised. These concern a great variety of areas of life. Sometimes the answers have come speedily, but at other times I have had to wait, or conclude that some particular prayer is not going to be answered. For over several decades, I have sought to pray that one particular unconverted person would come to faith in Christ, but as yet he shows not even a glimmer of spiritual interest. So, I pray on!

My prayer times begin with thanks, praise and worship. Then I need to confess my sins – naming them where I can – and ask for the blood of the Lord Jesus to wash me and make me whiter than snow.

I have my own prayer notebook containing lists of people and needs for which I pray. For some I pray daily, for others occasionally, and some are listed to be prayed for once each week. On Sunday, my focus is on churches and ministers I know. On Monday, I pray for missionaries and needy nations. On Tuesday I pray for evangelists and missioners working in the U.K. On Wednesday, I pray particularly for the nation, our governments, the media and educational establishments. On Thursday, I pray much for unconverted people, and unsaved children of Christian parents. On Friday, I have lists of names of friends and supporters whom I delight to bring to the Lord, and on Saturday I bring before the Lord cities and areas of great spiritual barrenness.

Every day I pray that God would lead me to someone with whom I can share the gospel. I deliberately go into the world on the lookout to chat with people who need to be introduced to the Lord Jesus. I am amazed at how frequently the Lord opens up conversations from inconsequential chatter to significant conversations that count for eternity.

As well as using my own words to pray, I sometimes use prayers written by others. I greatly appreciate the devotional writings of Kenneth Boa. Sometimes I pray the Litany, which is so helpful. It is photocopied in my own prayer diary. I usually pray the 'Lord's Prayer' before going to sleep each night.

Though I sometimes go on prayer walks, where I walk and pray out loud, and I often sit to pray, I have a purpose made prayer kneeler. It helps me truly set aside time 'to do business' with the Lord. However, probably my best times of prayer have been in prayer meetings. A group praying together, so that each prayer is not only valuable in itself, but a stimulant for further prayer means that a lengthy time of prayer can be a thorough covering of issues in depth. A good, lengthy time of corporate prayer is, for me, one of the great blessings and joys of being a Christian. Interestingly, so many of the promises in Scripture regarding answered prayer are relating to people praying together. A prayer meeting can be as edifying and thrilling as a great preaching event, so it bewilders me that they have fallen by the way in many Christian circles.

Prayer for me is the barometer of my spiritual life. It is the greatest joy, but it never just happens. I have to decide to pray, and make myself continue in prayer, but there is such spiritual happiness in being able to praise and pray to a Heavenly Father who delights to commune with me. What a privilege!

Rona Matheson

Rona Matheson grew up on the west coast of Scotland and now lives near Inverness with her husband and four daughters. As a young nanny abroad she became a Christian and then went on to work with Blythswood Care in Romania. She enjoys serving the Lord through family life and working with various women's ministries through church and conferences.

I didn't pray with any belief or conviction that it would make any difference until I prayed to God to forgive me my sins and for Jesus to come into my life at 22 years old. I knew from that first prayer, I had been heard and that God answered me. I received a peace that I knew was not of myself, as at that time I was in a very difficult situation. I remember being amazed God had answered me. I had also asked in that first prayer for a Bible that I may learn more about Jesus and the very next morning I was given one as a gift without having mentioned it to anyone. I think there is no greater incentive to pray than seeing answer to prayer! So having had such answers so clearly and instantly I began to pray more and more just talking to God asking for Him to teach me in His word. The words of the Bible seemed to come to life and so the more I read, the more I had to pray about.

Through His Word I quickly learned God had a plan for me and this made me pray for guidance. I had a decision to make about my future, to continue working abroad as a nanny and stay with my new church life or go back home, where I had led a very different lifestyle. One night on my knees I prayed, 'God show me what to do. If I go home I will be alone, no Christian friends and no help, but here I have a new life. I am happy to stay.' His words directed me, 'Go home and tell what God has done for you' (Mark 5:19). That was it. I had to go back to Scotland and tell I was a Christian. I got nervous and felt weak and then God spoke again, "I will never leave you or forsake you" (Heb. 13:5). I couldn't disobey. I had peace and in going back I got a job right away and a flat with a Christian and lots more I could never have imagined.

Prayer is the means by which God asks us to come to Him and for which He comes to us. I have never doubted God hears me. I am so thankful for wise and early teaching that gave me the assurance that God always hears, but does not always answer as we wish or hope for. I soon learned that our sin can hinder our prayer life, if not confessed and dealt with. It is easy to pray for change in our circumstances or in other people's lives when actually it is me that needs to be changing.

How wonderful to see answers to prayers of Christians who have gone before us. I was remembering the persecuted Church in Eastern European countries; and how many Christians prayed for these oppressed lands under communism for many years. This came home to me when I received my grandmother's Bible after her death. In it was a prayer for the persecuted church in Eastern Europe and its release from dictatorship. My grandmother had gone to glory before witnessing the fall of communism and also before seeing me, her granddaughter, go out to serve God in Romania and worship with the believers where once it was not permitted to take a Bible over their borders. This reminds me, we may not always see God's answers in this life, but God always hears and answers in ways we couldn't have imagined. It is also a reminder of how important it is to keep praying for Christians who face persecution in lands today. Also to pray always for loved ones who are outside His kingdom.

Prayer is not a burden, but I have found the more I neglect reading His Word the more I neglect prayer. But God knows we face these difficulties as He has said, 'The Spirit himself intercedes for us with groans that words cannot express'

(Rom. 8:26). How exciting it is to pray for our daily bread as taught in the Lord's Prayer and have it answered. Receiving through someone's kind act of giving a timely meal, a gift of their time or money, knowing only God knew your need.

We have an 11-year-old daughter, Sarah. She has been suffering with a rare epileptic syndrome for over six years now, where she can often be overcome with hundreds of seizures in a day. It has been frightening to have had so many emergency trips to hospital. We have prayed for her healing. We believe God hears us and, although she is not healed, we know His plan is greater than we can ask for in our prayers, as the Bible tells us, His plan is good (Rom. 8:28). We have been humbled by the many people who pray for Sarah here and abroad. We received a treatment for Sarah that wasn't available in the Highlands at the time she needed it. This treatment prevented brain damage. We received funding for this in direct answer to prayer. We continue to experience peace and strength and joy beyond ourselves in answer to so many people praying for us and as we face uncertainty with Sarah's health we hold onto God's promises. Because He who promises is faithful.

This hymn says wonderfully what prayer means to me:

What a friend we have in Jesus,
All our sins and griefs to bear,
What a privilege to carry,
Everything to God in prayer,
Oh what peace we often forfeit,
Oh what needless pain we bear,
All because we do not carry,
Everything to God in prayer.
Joseph Scriven, 1855

Ruth Box

Ruth Box became a Christian at the age of 6. After working in a bank for thirteen years, she has spent the rest of her working life to date serving with Christian mission agencies, and is presently Mobiliser for Scotland for AIM International. She is a member of Kirkintilloch Baptist Church, is single, sings a lot (in churches as well as in the bath!) and is yet another avid fan of 'The West Wing'.

People often say that prayer is hard work. And it can be. Sometimes – especially when we don't think we're getting any answers, or when we are in a spiritual battle – it can feel as if we are hammering on heaven's door and no one is home. But for me, I have to admit that for most of my life I've worked on a simple 'Father-Daughter' principle – if I want to know the answer to something, I ask my heavenly Dad. I'm not very good at big, theological prayers that use 'all the right words' – I just blether away to the One who knows me best and trust Him to tell me what I need to know. That does not necessarily mean that He tells me all I *want* to know, however!

I guess we all struggle from time to time with working out what God would have us do, especially when it comes to the 'big stuff' – should I go to university, what job should I do, should I change job, whom should I marry, should I marry at all?

There came a point in my life when I had not one, but four job offers on the table – all in what we call 'full-time Christian ministry', but in different agencies and in different parts of the world. One of these offers in particular felt like it could be the right way to go – I had been offered a role in the south of France working as PA to the director of a Christian organisation based there. I had a real heart for France and the French people, having been on a good number of short-term missions there in the past, to the extent that I would weep buckets on the ferry back to the U.K. each time I left. So I went to France to meet with the folks there in a fairly excited frame of mind, having said to God that I was happy to move or not move to France – I just needed to know from Him what He wanted me to do. Incredibly, the moment my feet touched the tarmac at the airport in France I knew without a doubt that I was in entirely the wrong place. It was a feeling I can't explain even to this day – I just *knew*. God had answered my prayer in a way I hadn't expected, but He had answered, and I was able to be secure in my decision to turn down the role and head back to Scotland.

Looking back, I think that one of the important things about prayer is that it builds our relationship with our heavenly Father. We learn to trust Him through prayer – through our on-going conversation with Him as the day to day routine of life progresses. When life doesn't turn out the way we had hoped, it is that relationship to which we cling. When everything around us is falling apart and we feel as if heaven is shut, we can only cling on to the faithfulness that God has shown to us in the past. We can know that He is with us, even when it doesn't feel like it at all, because we have experienced His presence with us in the past. Even more than with the best of earthly dads, I have found in my experience of prayer that I can cry out to Him in agony, celebrate in successes, be comforted in my despair and rest in His presence in times of stress.

Let me share another, more painful example. Around twelve years ago, God gave me a vision to reach out to young people who go clubbing in Glasgow city centre, and for the next ten years, I and a team of board members, volunteers and family members worked to raise funds, formulate plans, look for suitable premises and finally open a 24/7 café in the centre of the city. I gave up my job in preparation for running the venue and all seemed to be the fulfilment of God's direction those many years ago. As we prepared the premises for opening day, however, we began to realise that the figures were just not stacking up the way we had hoped they would. It very quickly became apparent that the café, in the format and venue we were setting up, was not going to be financially viable and we would have to close. The café was open for a grand total of five days. I was now unemployed, I felt that I had let lots of people down and that God had let me down.

Over the ensuing months, my world fell apart and the worst thing was the feeling I mentioned before of heaven being closed. I believe that there is no worse feeling for a child of God than to feel that one's Father is no longer listening. But of course, He was listening. He was with me through it all, just as He had promised. He was listening to my anguished cries for help, comfort and understanding, and now, two years on, I can understand a little of what He was teaching me through the trauma of that devastating period. As I serve Him now in the pastoral care of missionaries who work in Africa, I can understand a little of their struggle when they suffer hardship, cope with apparent failure and try to work through the aftermath of trauma. Without having learned personally how to take my agony to God and trust Him in the midst of the darkness, I would be less than useful to those on the mission field who are suffering now.

Prayer is a conversation. It is the way my relationship with God grows. It can be hard work. It can be a joy. It is always a privilege. It should be as vital as breathing, as nourishing as food and as refreshing as spring water on a hot day. It is how my Dad and I communicate – as simple and as complex as that.

Stephen Barton

Stephen has been a Christian since he was 15 after a friend shared the gospel with him. He is married to Joy and has two little girls, Hannah and Bethan. He is a graduate of Highland Theological College and a prospective minister with the Fellowship of Independent Evangelical Churches. He lives in Inverness and is a member of Culloden Baptist Church.

Since becoming a Christian at 15, prayer has been a normal part of my life, normal not in a mundane sense but in a necessary sense, normal like breathing. Every day, all day I pray different types of prayers. First thing every morning I pray asking God to help me understand His WORD and to change me through it. At meal times alone or with my family, putting the girls to bed or last thing at night prayer is part of every day. Then there are those times throughout the day when I just want to share part of what's going on with God, or I need his help. I've learnt over the years that I can pray silent short prayers whilst out and about. As God is everywhere I can pray wherever I go and He'll hear me.

Prayer is important to me because I know God hears my prayers. I know this even though at times it feels like my prayers are hitting the ceiling. I know it because that's what it says in my Bible, I know it because the Spirit often confirms it, but I also know it from experience.

I can't remember not praying. I didn't grow up in a Christian home and was never taught to pray, but I would pray every night before I went to sleep. I do remember the first time I was sure

God heard my prayer, I was standing on a bridge in the north of Wales and had just had the gospel explained to me. At that point I knew I wasn't a Christian but I prayed and asked God to forgive me and though there was no flashing lights, I did begin to feel alive inside, I had never felt empty but now felt full. I had never felt dirty, but I now felt clean. I had zero Bible knowledge but it felt like I was a brand new person, like I had been born again.

Since then I have had specific answers to prayer that point to God's faithfulness and his ability to answer prayer. Take for instance the time I prayed for a wife. Now I had been praying for a wife for a number of years with no answer. On the 14th of February one year I came home from work and found there was no Valentine day's card and I let out a big sigh and called out to God, 'Where is she, Lord?' I realised then I was addressing the Lord of all things and so I prayed something like this, 'Lord I have waited and there is no sign of a wife, couldn't I communicate with her before my 30th birthday.'

I gave God two weeks to answer this specific prayer: Later that day I was checking my e-mails and I had an e-mail from J. Barton, thinking it was from my dad and that he had finally worked out how to send an e-mail I opened it. It turned out to be from someone called Joy. Joy said in her e-mail, 'I just thought I'd let you know that it is Pastor Chris's birthday today – God bless, Joy.' Whilst it might not sound like a thrilling e-mail, I wondered if it was an answer to my prayer and I was excited. I e-mailed back and said, 'I am not the person you were looking for but I do have a pastor and I am a Christian'. I got an email back politely apologising as she thought my e-mail address was her brother's. As I had my prayer in the back of my mind and the thought that just because she has a pastor doesn't mean she's a Christian, so I sent another e-mail asking, 'What is saving faith?' She responded with a gospel message that was clear and concise and left a challenge, 'What about you?' So I sent back a gospel message from Genesis. This was the start of an e-mail relationship, but I had also found out that she lived in the U.S. some four thousand miles away so I assumed that this was not an answer to my prayer, so I put the prayer to the back of my mind.

Over the next few months we developed a stronger relationship as we were so far apart we could share anything, soon e-mails turned to phone calls and the phone calls became longer and more frequent. Still she lived 4,000 miles away and that is a long way to go for a blind date. God would have it different though as Joy's younger brother Tim took a year out to work for a mission organisation and they sent him to London. In the October I got a call from Joy saying her whole family were coming to London in December so they could see Tim as he would be away for Christmas. So on December 5th at 12.00 I got off a train in Euston and met Joy and her whole family. Joy said goodbye to her family for the day and we went out and about London. When we visited the British Museum I was getting excited about one of the Pharaohs and started to go on a bit. I stopped and decided to apologise and as I looked into her beautiful brown eyes I remembered my prayer and knew that we were going to get married. My next thought was not to tell her otherwise I might scare her away. The next day we spent another wonderful day together, but there was a touch of sadness as I was going home. However, I also knew that this was just the start. As the train pulled away that day it felt like a separation that shouldn't happen. We didn't see each other again until the following summer but we were on the phone more often. When summer arrived I travelled to the U.S. and Joy came back with me. On the final week of her visit we got engaged. I told Joy my story and she had a similar story all the way along. When God is your matchmaker it is thrilling to enjoy the romance. On the 7th of June 2003 we got married and we have been blessed as we go through all the different circumstances of life together and with our God who hears our prayers.

I have learned and I am probably still learning that sometimes the answer to our prayers is no, and that's ok too. Prayer is communication with my loving heavenly Father. He and He alone knows what is best for me. I have also learned the best thing I get from prayer is not that God answers all my requests but that He is there for me to talk to and He uses prayer as a means to transform me to become more like Him and to love Him more. I have learnt that prayer in difficult times can lead to a peace that goes beyond all understanding. I have also found that as wonderful as my relationship is with the wife God has given me, my relationship with Him is even better.

Steve Brady

Steve Brady is Principal of Moorlands College, a trustee of the Keswick Convention, an author and much-travelled preacher. He is married to Brenda, has two children, three grandchildren, loves sport, hates gardening and has an irrational attachment to Everton Football Club. He has entitled his article: 'Help, Lord!'

A wise counsellor challenged my laid-back address to the Almighty when, as a seventeen-year old, I was trying to get some quick-fire help for some problem or other in my life. He simply said, 'You'll need to be far more desperate with God, Steve!'

Years later, I heard a missionary say words to the effect that one of the Christian's greatest strategies in prayer is desperation! A cursory reading of the Psalms, with their frequent cries to the Lord for help, would quickly confirm that observation. Why desperation? Why the cry, 'Help, Lord!'?

First, I find prayer to be the polar opposite to my proud, stubborn self-sufficiency. It is not wrong or sinful to be competent and accomplished. The Bible reminds us that whatever we do, we should do it heartily for the Lord (see Col. 3:23, for example). But somewhere in the dark recesses of my heart is a belief and conviction that I can do it my way; I can cope; I can succeed; I can be self-sufficient. It is that spirit of independence from God not dependence on him. So there are times when I realise I am simply relying on myself not the Lord. And when I am, there lurks unbelief, the seedbed of all sin ('Did God really say?' – check out Genesis 3). Then some emergency or problem arises, and I am flummoxed. But the Lord has my attention now. As C.S. Lewis reminds us, 'God whispers to us in our pleasures... but shouts in our pains: it is His megaphone to rouse a deaf world.' Now I am listening, calling for help. That's how and why and where prayer strips me bare, showing me who I am, a person in need of real grace, deep down in the core of my being. For me, to keep that attitude of total dependence on the Lord, nothing seems more appropriate than a genuine, 'Help, Lord!'

Why appropriate? Just think about the situation for a moment. How can anyone really come into the presence of a God who is 'holy, holy, holy,' and knows all the nooks and crannies of our souls? Dare we think that we can live a life that pleases him when we are told that without Jesus, we can't? Where did we get and then harbour the idea that God would be impressed by our gifts, wisdom, experience, and social and family connections? Am I in danger of thinking myself indispensable, as if the Triune God needed to adjunct me into the Godhead to accomplish his purposes? 'Help, Lord!'

Such questions have taught me the need for various forms of desperation. At its most basic, I know I need the Lord Jesus both as my Lord and my mediator. So, one of the great secrets of prayer is found in the phrase, 'we have confidence to enter the Most Holy Place by the blood of Jesus', that is, through the merits of his death for us (Heb. 10:19 NIV). Whether I am having 'a great day', whatever that means, or a 'bad hair' one and feeling about as spiritual as a plate of spam sandwiches, I need to remind myself that because of Jesus I may always come to my Father, inspired and energised by the Holy Spirit. So I seek to start there – with the God who invites me into his presence, an invitation provided at immeasurable cost. Worship, praise and thanksgiving become the accompanying friends to my, 'Help, Lord!'

But then I have a whole agenda of people, projects, and this, that and the other for me to see, decide, do and accomplish – and that is before prayer letters and requests drop into my e-mail box or I consult the indispensable *Operation World.*

'Help, Lord, where do I begin?' Here I need some organisation to my prayer life. So, some people I pray for over and over again – family, friends, colleagues, students etc. Some are facing huge challenges in their lives through no fault of their own, like my wife who suffers from Multiple Sclerosis, and they just need strength to get through another day. Others have made bad choices and continue to stray away from the God who can fix them. All of them need to know the gospel, love it and share it, not just those who are in 'full-time' Christian work. Practically, for many years, I used a daily, weekly and monthly list of people for whom to pray. When pastor of a local church, with many hundreds in the congregation, this was the only way I could systematically intercede for each member and their families. And what of the myriad of duties that confront me? Decisions about whether this course of action is good or that one is better; lectures to write and preaching to prepare for and deliver; crises and emergencies that no-one can predict arise and can tear my heart apart. How appropriate is a desperate, 'Help, Lord!'

One of the great prayers in the Bible is found on the lips of the fifth-century BC rebuilder of ancient Jerusalem, Nehemiah. A small Hebrew word is used a number of times in his prayer recorded in chapter one. For example, a couple of times it is translated as 'I beseech' in the *King James Version*. It is one way, facing a 'big ask' before King Artaxerxes, that Nehemiah can put his whole problem into perspective. He needs so much to rebuild a city – just think about it! And before that he needs the king to change his mind on a previous decree that stopped the rebuilding work a few years before. But he knows there is a higher throne, with the King of Kings upon it, so he desperately asks the eternal King for what he needs, confessing his helplessness, before he lays his request before Artaxerxes. In his classic book, *Prayer,* O. Hallesby says: 'Helplessness becomes prayer the moment you go to Jesus and speak candidly and confidently with him about your needs.' When we do, we discover that 'Help, Lord!' soon becomes a 'Thank you, Lord!' And, as I sign off, and not knowing you or your circumstances, my prayer for you is appropriately straightforward: 'Help, Lord!'

Wallace Benn

The Right Reverend Wallace Benn was Bishop of Lewes from 1997-2012. As well as being an experienced parish minister he is a well-known inspirational teacher, speaker and a published author. Wallace is President of the Church of England Evangelical Council and Chairman of Bible by the Beach. He is an enthusiastic rugby and motor racing watcher and supporter.

I well remember my first answer to prayer! I was about seven years old and we had moved to the country, so I asked my Dad if I could have a pony. He wisely said – 'When you are a bit older'. Not to be put off I asked for a donkey instead! My dad was cautious but I started praying for one. Imagine my joy when after lunch one Sunday a donkey walked up our driveway and just stood outside the door! He was never claimed and I had him with delight until he died.

Jesus makes it clear in the Upper Room discourse that prayer and joy are deeply connected. 'Until now you have asked nothing in my name. Ask, and you will receive, that your joy may be full (John 16:24 ESV).' God is omniscient, He knows everything, so He doesn't need our prayers. But He sometimes withholds blessing until we ask so that we may have the joy of answered prayer. He wonderfully includes us in the working out of His Sovereign purposes. Prayer is more for our benefit than His, though He delights in the relationship developed with His children through prayer and reading His Word. 'He ordained it not so much for His own sake as for ours.' (John Calvin from his wonderful section on Prayer; Book 3, Chapter 20 of The Institutes).

We need to understand the privilege of prayer more than the often emphasised duty of prayer. I have a plaque on my wall given me when I was made a bishop. It says, I am the Queen's 'well beloved Wallace'. Just imagine me clutching that at Buckingham Palace and asking to pop in and see the Queen for a chat! Yet I can talk to the King of kings at any time of day wherever I am and know that He hears as my heavenly Father – what a privilege!

Jesus taught that prayer need not be long or repetitious or 'posh' (see Matt 6:7-8). It ought to be a respectful, amazed and delightful conversation with our heavenly Father. As Hannah learned in difficult circumstances it is a 'pouring out of my soul before the Lord' and it often lifts a sadness of spirit (1 Sam. 1:15,18 ESV). It above all needs to be real and heart felt.

It also needs to be God centred as we learn to pray in line with God's revealed will and submit to His providential directing of our lives. When I look back on my life as a committed Christian (now over fifty years), I am not only thankful for the many prayers wonderfully answered in so many ways but also for some key prayers God did not answer – He had kinder, better or more helpful things in mind for me and my family than I knew or asked for! And even in the hard times we can trust that in the end 'all things work together for good' for those who love God (Rom. 8:28 ESV). I have had to learn the hard way that what I think is good (the gift of a Ferrari!) is not necessarily in my best interest 'to be conformed to the image of His Son' which is God's ultimate purpose for His redeemed children! (Rom. 8:29 ESV).

Prayer for the Christian should be as natural as breathing! Jesus commends private prayer away from public gaze (Matt 6:6). 'What a man is on his knees before God, that he is and no more' (Robert Murray McCheyne) is a profound and right comment. But we are also to 'pray without ceasing' (1 Thess 5:17 ESV) and to 'practice the presence of the Lord' with us through each new day and in each new challenge or opportunity. Also the prayers of others sustain and help us maybe when we find it difficult to pray (Phil. 1:19 ESV).

When my son was twelve, on the run-up to Christmas he came and asked if I was in a good mood. When I said, 'yes of course', he mentioned the mountain bike we had seen in a window recently. He added, 'I've been thinking about it and if I saved all my pocket money by the time I could afford it, I'd be too old to enjoy it! Dad if it's alright with you could I just have it?' What was my son doing? He was expressing his dependence on his father and his own lack of resources to cope with what was needed. Prayer is the best expression of our dependence upon God. When we don't pray we are really saying we can live the Christian life and do what is right by our own resources, and that's folly!

I was told as a young Christian to pray home all the promises of God to His children in His Word that were relevant to me or to others that God had placed on my heart. I was also wisely advised to pray for, or about, things your mind wanders off to! I have recently been delighting in praying through a Psalm each day. Sheer joy (and challenge!).

What a friend we have in Jesus,
All our sins and griefs to bear!
What a privilege to carry
Everything to God in prayer!
Oh, what peace we often forfeit,
Oh, what needless pain we bear,
All because we do not carry
Everything to God in prayer!
　　(Hymn by Joseph M. Scriven 1855)

Peace is forfeited and pain caused by a lack of prayer in a believer's life. Let's make the most of the gracious and unde-served friendship of our Saviour to us! As has been said 'Six prayerless days makes one weak!'

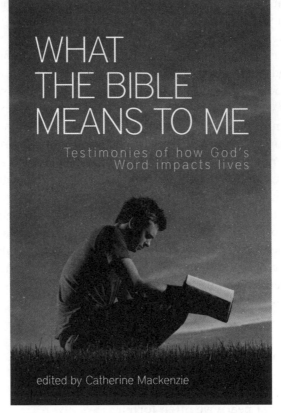

WHAT THE BIBLE MEANS TO ME
Testimonies of how God's Word impacts lives
edited by Catherine Mackenzie

From all backgrounds, nationalities and cultures people are re-markably different, but also intriguingly the same. God's Word has something to say to all mankind and in this book forty-five people summarise what the Bible means to them. The bus driver and the theologian; the missionary and the midwife; the army chaplain and the artist. We know how different they are, but we also see their similarities ... their search for truth; their need for love; their quest for faith. Through the Word of God we can see how God loves us, faithfully and truly and how his Word is a Word for all times and ages. It's a Word for you.

ISBN 978-1-84550-723-7

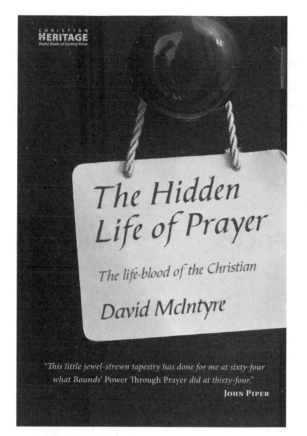

THE HIDDEN LIFE OF PRAYER
The life-blood of the Christian
David McIntyre

'God brings books at their appointed times. *The Hidden Life of Prayer* arrived late but well-timed. This little jewel-strewn tapestry has done for me at 64 what Bounds' Power Through Prayer did at 34. I could be ashamed that I need inspiration for the highest privilege. But I choose to be thankful.'

John Piper, founder and teacher of desiringGod.org

Drawing on the experiences of people like Luther, Spurgeon, Muller, Whitefield and Wesley, the author presses the case for a greater commitment to prayer. His advice may not only transform your life, it could be a catalyst towards a change in the world around you.

ISBN 978-1-84550-586-8

Christian Focus Publications

Our mission statement –

STAYING FAITHFUL
In dependence upon God we seek to impact the world through literature faithful to His infallible Word, the Bible. Our aim is to ensure that the Lord Jesus Christ is presented as the only hope to obtain forgiveness of sin, live a useful life and look forward to heaven with Him.

Our Books are published in four imprints:

CHRISTIAN
FOCUS

CHRISTIAN
HERITAGE

Popular works including biographies, commentaries, basic doctrine and Christian living.

Books representing some of the best material from the rich heritage of the church.

MENTOR

CF4·K

Books written at a level suitable for Bible College and seminary students, pastors, and other serious readers. The imprint includes commentaries, doctrinal studies, examination of current issues and church history.

Children's books for quality Bible teaching and for all age groups: Sunday school curriculum, puzzle and activity books; personal and family devotional titles, biographies and inspirational stories – Because you are never too young to know Jesus!

Christian Focus Publications Ltd,
Geanies House, Fearn, Ross-shire,
IV20 1TW, Scotland, United Kingdom.
www.christianfocus.com